SILICON SPIES

SILICON SPIES

Lauran Paine

St. Martin's Press
New York

Library of Congress Cataloging in Publication Data

Paine, Lauran.
  Silicon spies.

  1. Espionage, Russian—United States.
2. Munitions—United States. 3. Business intelligence—United
States. 4. Technology transfer—Soviet Union.
5. Technology transfer—United States. I. Title.
UB271.R9P35 1987   327.1′2′0947   86-24837
ISBN 0-312-00183-5

First published in Great Britain by Robert Hale Limited.

First U.S. Edition

10 9 8 7 6 5 4 3 2 1

Contents

SILICON SPIES

1

The Kennan Memorandum

Throughout the first week of May 1983 the international Press reported that midget Soviet submarines were operating in the waters off the strategic port of Sundsvall in Sweden, as well as in the deep coastal sea of Hardangerfjord off Norway's west coast.

In one Norwegian incident sonar contact was made at 7.21 p.m. on 23 April 1983 by the Navy frigate *Oslo* which, after ascertaining that no friendly submarines were in the area, engaged in anti-submarine operations. The search lasted five days, during which time Norwegian submarines, a patrol aircraft and four warships were involved in the hunt. On 3 May the search was terminated; the foreign submarine had escaped.

During the Swedish incursion Premier Olaf Palme neither called for NATO assistance nor permitted a concerted search. His orders were to 'Avoid any incident.'

Two months earlier, in March 1983, a Soviet flotilla including service vessels, submarines and the aircraft-carrier *Kiev* spent a week in manoeuvres off both Stockholm and Malmö.

Since 1969 Norway had reported more than 130 Soviet violations of her territorial waters and Sweden approximately a hundred since 1980.

Although Soviet naval activity is not new in the waters of Scandinavia, going back as far as 1962, since 1980 it has increased considerably and has appeared to have a pattern which has less to do with manoeuvres than it has to do with inshore soundings. If, as US Secretary of the Navy John F. Lehman Jr, said, Soviet plans in the event of war are to overrun Norway early on in order to 'operate submarine wolf packs the way the Germans did in World War II ...', then inshore plotting would be necessary. But the use of crawler-type mini-submarines for this purpose was a surprise to Swedish and Norwegian defence authorities. According to the chief of the Swedish Defence Command, the Soviet Union had managed to hide the existence of its crawler-submarines from Western Intelligence.

During the autumn of 1982 foreign submarines manoeuvred off Stockholm, and one crawler-submarine approached within a mile of the city. The Swedish Submarine Defence Commission obtained underwater photographs of the tracks of this submarine, and Vice-Admiral Bror Stefenson reported that the mini-crawlers '... were a surprise to us'.

But in other quarters they were not a surprise. Miles Costick, a Yugoslavian-born US citizen in the employ of an American organization which monitors sales of American technology to foreign interests, told a US national strategy conference in Washington that during 1975 a US company exported crawler-submarines to the Soviet Union through Zurich in violation of US export restrictions. Three of these vessels, deep-diving Pisces-type submersibles originally developed for undersea pipeline-laying and oil exploration, were constructed of a special alloy which would withstand great pressure at considerable depths. Because of export restrictions by both the US and Canadian governments several of these vessels were manufactured in Britain, dismantled and shipped to Zurich for re-assembly and delivery to the Soviet Union.

They were examples of the extensive leaks – the haemorrhage – of Western technology which has been largely responsible for the immense progress of Soviet military technology over the last forty years.

They were also examples of the West's confusion over what is exportable and what is not, and how some individuals and companies have contributed to the growth and capability of a hostile military system the West must now spend approximately 34.7 per cent of its Gross National Product (GNP) to defend itself against, with both totals increasing steadily; the amount of Western technology reaching the Soviet Union and the amount of the West's

GNP being funnelled into defence against a system its own technology has largely created.

In 1972 world military expenditures, of which the US and the USSR are the largest spenders, stood at $300 billion. In 1982 the total was $820 billion. In 1984 it was $970 billion. In 1985 it passed the one trillion mark. The size of this sum can perhaps be more readily grasped if it is related to national indebtedness. If the last figure is employed, the national debts among developed countries would be erased in one decade.

This situation exists because Western technology has been allowed to reach the Soviet Union as a result of both ignorance and duplicity.

The Soviet Union is an authoritarian state which historically has been unable to achieve either commercial or military parity with the West unless it can acquire Western technology. For the last fifty years it has been a military power, and although such items as the Pisces-type crawler-submarines may not have originally been developed to serve military ends, in the Soviet Union, no such distinction exists. Where necessary every technical development the USSR has acquired from the West has been altered, first to serve military requirements and secondly to serve the civilian sector.

Beginning with Vladimir Lenin and continuing through to the Soviet leadership of Mikhail Gorbachev, Russia has been a military-oriented state. As long as military requirements conformed to the necessity all countries share of being able to defend themselves, the Russian build-up was reasonable and understandable. But when any nation, the Soviet Union today or National Socialist Germany fifty years ago, exceeds its defensive needs, it follows a policy of aggressive intentions.

It is not the custom of nations to accumulate a vast arsenal for window-dressing; they do so because they intend to use their arsenals for the only purpose for which weapons exist. As Bismarck said, you can do anything with bayonets but sit on them.

Without advanced acquisitions from the West, Soviet technology, at least in the past, has been incapable of achieving industrial or military parity. Between the Russian Revolution and the Second World War the USSR's hermetic insularity coupled to its anaemic economy prevented it from achieving even a rudimentary scientific or technological sector. After the Second World War it established a goal of parity with the West based upon acquisition of Western technology by whatever means were required to ensure success. For the Russians this meant every advanced device or technique developed in the free world but predominantly those which possessed military significance. In order to achieve this goal they created an enormous bureaucracy and honed it to a high degree of efficiency for the next forty years. There has never been anything like it before. Its successes must certainly have surpassed the expectations of its founders, its acquisitions have required the development of other bureaucracies whose purpose is to adapt and enhance its acquisitions.

A Texas company which manufactures seismographic equipment for oil exploration sold its products to the Soviet Union. This equipment is presently being used to detect and pinpoint the location of NATO submarines. Two huge floating dry docks manufactured in Sweden and Japan were obtained by the Soviet Union to service its trawler fleet. They are presently servicing Soviet warships, including the aircraft-carrier *Kiev*.

Shortly before the beginning of the present decade, at the time of the free world's development of high-technology computer science, the Soviet drive to acquire Western technology increased considerably. An Intelligence projection, which was subsequently proved to be low, estimated that at least 275 Soviet experts serving in United Nations positions or in diplomatic positions in the United States were in the country solely to buy, steal or through espionage and bribery acquire such US high-tech items as lasers, computer products, cryogenic, fusion, image-processing design and retrieval, pattern-recognition, programming, instantaneous sighting and firing products, or their specifications and blueprints. Although this raiding has increased tremendously since 1970 and has been ongoing for forty years and has resulted in the creation of the Soviet military capability as it exists today, and also despite abundant evidence that Western leaders have known that the USSR has never deviated from its goal of armed superiority over the West, the flow of Western technology going eastward has increased rather than decreased over the last ten years. In 1929 an officer of the Revolutionary Military Soviet said: 'We must ... ensure that industry can as quickly as possible be adapted to serve military needs ... It is necessary to plan for duplication of technological processes and absorb foreign assistance.' Fifteen years later, in 1944, a US State Department official, George Kennan, wrote in a memorandum that it was not '... our lack of knowledge which causes us to be puzzled by Russia. It is that we are incapable of understanding the truth about Russia when we see it.' Twenty-eight years later US Secretary of Commerce Maurice Stans confirmed the accuracy of the Kennan Memorandum when he said that, 'History has shown that when there is increasing trade between countries ... there is a tendency toward increasing understanding.'

The Kennan Memorandum had stood the test of time. During the intervening years neither the US government nor Maurice Stans had learned anything, and the US government still has not. Present US Secretary of State George Schultz, in an address before the House Foreign Affairs Committee given on 9 February 1984, said that, 'The instrumentalities of foreign assistance are potent and essential tools that advance our interests.' At the very time of that address, technical translators of the Soviet State Committee for Science and Technology (GKNT) had in their possession more than 1.5 million scientific papers from 124 nations from which they could identify technological advances suitable for Soviet military adaptability, nearly all this information gained through foreign assistance organizations in the West.

In 1966 the US Senator from New York, Jacob Javits, said that, 'Trade with the west ? must necessarily be a marginal factor in the performances and potentialities of the Soviet economy,' despite the fact that by 1966 there was overwhelming evidence that this simply was not true. Five years later a Soviet official, Konstantin Krylov, stated that everything acquired from the West as well as all labour in the Soviet Union which had any bearing on '... national economic planning is inseparably tied to national defence requirements'.

At roughly the same time – 1971 – it was stated by the London-born US citizen Anthony Sutton, a former professor of economics and Research Fellow at the Hoover Institution, that, 'One of the great successes of Soviet planning has been the priority diversion of resources to armaments production and the associated militarization of industrial sectors.'

By 1971 the word 'defence' when applied to the Soviet Union had become a euphemism, and George Bernard Shaw's question: 'What on earth is the true faith of an armourer?' had been answered by the USSR when it continued to refer to its military establishments as 'defensive' when it had achieved superiority over its avowed enemies in the air, on land and at sea in all categories but one: aircraft-carriers.

The true faith of history's most overly-armed nation was conquest. In 1971 an article in *Krasnaya Zuezda*, official periodical of the Red Army, stated: 'All of heavy industry – from steel to electronics – and not only the pure defence industries producing military end products, represent the foundation of [Soviet] power.'

The Soviet system is and has been a military, war-footing complex whose diversion of resources from within the country and acquisitions from beyond the national borders have for fifty years operated on a military-priority basis. It has not been geared to defence in fifteen years but rather to either covert or overt aggression, and so thoroughly has the socio-political structure of the nation been subjugated to that objective that the USSR with an economy half that of the United States has been able to equal and surpass the US in military production.

Krylov has noted that not less than seventy-five per cent of the Soviet Union's resources'... are spent by the armed forces for the purchase of armaments', a figure considerably in excess of actual defence requirements. But that figure would not have provided parity without the acquisition of

Western technology. During World War II Soviet armies were still using World War I machine-guns, horse-drawn caissons and the tactics of Tannenberg which in 1914 cost them 300,000 men.

Without the subsequent acquisition of Western technology Russia would certainly have made progress between the world wars and afterwards, but the Soviets never could have achieved parity without it, particularly once sophisticated weaponry appeared in the free world, and obviously they knew this was true, otherwise it is inconceivable that they would have mounted such a monolithic effort to plunder the West of high technology.

Everything Soviet agents acquired in the West could be used directly or could be converted for military purposes including items Western officials have categorically stated could not be used that way. An example would be the aluminum powder plant erected under the supervision of an American engineer, W. Hahn, in the Soviet Union. It was stated that aluminum powder had no military use, when in fact aluminum powder is a requisite for increasing the explosive capability of ammunition.

Even farm products, which, aside from their obvious value of keeping the workers who produce military hardware well-fed and healthy, can be and are used in the production of such war material as bombs, automotive spare parts, fuel and plastics.

Another example would be the huge Gorki automobile factory built with official US sanction in the Soviet Union under the aegis of the Ford Motor Company which agreed to provide technical assistance, along with two other US industrial firms, Brown Lipe Gear Company and Timken-Detroit Axle Company. This factory was completed in 1933 and that same year started production of military vehicles. During World War II Ford-Gorki produced half-track troop-carriers. After the war Ford-Gorki specialized in amphibious troop-carriers. By 1950 the factory was producing improved versions of the same armoured amphibious carrier, plus additional military hardware, and by 1960 it was producing armoured carriers capable of transporting troops and heavy cargo, as well as field howitzers, rocket-launchers and wire-guidance anti-tank missile systems.

During an address in 1967, Soviet Premier Leonid Brezhnev said: 'You know well, comrades, that the Soviet Union is rendering great economic, military and political assistance to ... [North] Vietnam.' One year later American and Allied losses during the Vietnam War reached their peak. That same year US equipment was still being shipped to the Gorki factory for use in the production of military equipment which, when completed, was sent to North Vietnam.

In both the Korean and Vietnamese wars Soviet-supplied T-34 and PT-26 tanks used against American and Allied soldiers rode on US suspension systems and tracks from Caterpillar Tractor Company designs. Roughly eighty per cent of Soviet military aid in both wars was either of US manufacture or from designs furnished to the Soviet Union through the policies of succeeding US administrations having to do with transfers of US technology.

Estimated total Allied casualties during the Korean War were 995,601. The estimated total Allied casualties during the Vietnam War were 158,000. Except for a significantly small percentage of those casualties, every one was a result of free-world participation in the creation of the Soviet war-making capability.

During the slaughter-house year of the Vietnam War, 1967, the same year Leonid Brezhnev stated that his country was aiding North Vietnam, US Secretary of State, Dean Rusk stated that helping the Soviet Union build, equip and operate the huge Volgorod factory, which would manufacture wheeled vehicles, was contributing to peace. Rusk said the Volgorod project had no military potential.

This installation, built between 1968 and 1971 and referred to as the 'Soviet-Fiat' automobile factory, is one of the largest factories in the world, with a capacity of 600,000 vehicles annually. Military equipment manufactured there has appeared in Syria, Lebanon and Cuba. It has also been exported to African and Central American leftist organizations. It has been an integral part of Soviet Union's total commitment to international insurrection and chaos, which in 1972 cost the USSR almost $300 million and which had by 1982 escalated to $900 million. The supervision, machine tools and Western technology which made the Volgorod installation operable came from the Hawker-Siddeley Dynamics Company of Great Britain, the Fiat Company of Italy, and no fewer than five major US industrial organizations.

2

Some Degrees of Failure

In 1921, two years before his death, Vladimir Ilyich Lenin (otherwise Ulyanov) said 'The capitalist countries ... will supply us with the materials and technology we lack ... which we need for our victorious attacks upon our suppliers ... they will work hard to prepare for their own suicide.' Since the year Lenin made that statement, free-world leaders have done their utmost to implement it.

In 1976 former US Secretary of State William Rogers reaffirmed the accuracy of the 1944 Kennan Memorandum and the earlier Lenin pronouncement when he said that trade agreements between the West and the Soviet Union would ensure a 'climate of peace'. One year later Britain's Anthony Wedgwood Benn signed agreements with the Soviet Union for technical assistance, and in 1978 British Prime Minister Harold Wilson, accompanied by James Callaghan, visited Moscow and shortly thereafter signed agreements which provided the USSR and Cuba with the financial and technical aid which was required for the conquest of Angola.

These events were consistent with US Secretary of State Henry Kissinger's 1975 statement that the West's goal was to advance the idea of mutual interests with the Soviet Union in order to encourage a tempering of Soviet aggressiveness, but the results were different, and one year later the bird which had been so protectively nurtured came home to roost. The Soviet Union possessed the preponderance of force in Europe, had the ability to disrupt NATO's sea lanes of supply and was out-producing NATO's most prominent member, the US, in aircraft, tanks, tactical weapons and submarines.

Britain's NATO envoy, Sir John Killick, thought: '...

something is amiss when the Soviet Union's all-consuming military machine continues to gather speed and strength ...'
It was probably reasonable to suspect that something was 'amiss'. Russia and her client states had established nearly eight hundred manufacturing ventures with Western industries all of which had a direct or end-product relationship to military use. For the USSR the critical fields were electronics, transportation, engineering, chemicals and construction; from Britain the USSR obtained a complete shipyard; from France a sophisticated chemical plant built at Orenburg in Central Russia; from Germany's ubiquitous Krupp *Konzern*, in conjunction with a smaller company, several coal-gasification installations. If anyone still had to be told, the goal of these acquisitions, in the words of a Soviet Intelligence officer, was to '... adapt them to the specifications of Soviet military production'.

An interesting sidelight of all this is that, since neither the Soviet Union nor its satellites are able to produce enough non-military goods for export sale to finance their expensive acquisitions of Western goods and services, they borrowed money in the West. By 1976 they owed in excess of $35 billion, considered in Western banking circles to be the limit of their credit. Between then and now, 1976 to 1985, that figure has more than doubled. Bearing in mind statements by Communist leaders including Josef Stalin that any way in which the USSR can weaken the West must be undertaken, then quite conceivably a repudiation of this debt would help to create the chaos Soviet leaders desire in the free-world.

Stalin also said that, '... about two-thirds of all the large industrial enterprises in the Soviet Union have been built with United States help or technical assistance'.

This is not quite accurate. French, Italian, German, Danish, Swedish, British and Japanese contributions were part of that two-thirds.

In every instance the two basic arguments employed to legitimize this one-way exchange were the same. The most common one was that if, for example, the US did not sell the products of its free society to the Soviet Union, it would buy them from other countries. The other argument was that either limited or unrestricted trade with the USSR of such 'non-military' items as wheeled vehicles, ships, machine tools, even synthetic, inorganic fertilizers, could not pose a threat to Western security.

The fallacy here is that everything people produce can be utilized for military purposes either directly or indirectly. With very little change the formulas for the production of chemical fertilizers can result in the production of synthetic fuels, explosives and poison gas. Two ordinarily harmless kitchen items, soap and sugar, when added to gasoline enhance the explosive power of bombs. If the intention is to exploit resources for military ends, then even Britain's recent clandestine exportation of butter to the Soviet Union through Rotterdam, fifty thousand tonnes (49,200 tons) of it, will serve a military purpose. This also applies to the sale of Danish commercial marine engines for use by the Soviet merchant fleet during the fifties and sixties. These engines powered the Soviet vessels which carried missiles to Cuba in 1962 when the US and the USSR came very close to war.

The degree to which the West can be deluded by these arguments, or can delude itself, was made evident by the viewpoint of the US Committee for Economic Development (CED) which advocated a ban on 'particularly useful' military products that did not include marine diesel engines because they were classified as 'merchant marine' equipment. This same viewpoint prevailed elsewhere. Precision machines and machine tools, the high-grade metals used throughout the West in the production of automobiles as well as ships, aircraft, tractors, fishing boats, trawlers and sea-going fish-processing vessels, were exempt from the CED ban.

One of these 'commercial' vessels, the *Labinsk*, 9,820 tons, powered by Italian Fiat engines, brought off the Soviet missiles from Cuba as deck cargo. The *Poltava*-class 'merchant' ships which had originally carried the missiles to Cuba were powered by Danish engines, either manufactured in Copenhagen or produced in the Soviet Union from Danish specifications provided through a 1959 technical assistance programme. The US approved of the Danish-Soviet arrangement because it was non-strategic.

A list of examples such as these would be almost endless, and the idea that unless the technologically advanced countries trade with the Soviets they will acquire what they need elsewhere is also only marginally accurate.

There are for example a number of large, precision manufacturing machines in the US no other country possesses. There are manufacturing techniques in Britain, the USA, France and Japan not available in other countries. In California's 'Silicon Valley' there are sophisticated electronic systems not even to be found in other areas of the United States. Many of the very advanced products the Soviets want most simply could not be obtained 'elsewhere'.

Conversely, items which could be classified as non-strategic such as cotton, sugar, wood pulp and ammonia become strategic if that is the intention of those who acquire them. A long list of items such as purified cellulose derived from cotton or wood pulp and cellulose end-products along with ethyl alcohol, concentrates of sulphuric and nitric acid, stable ammonia and ammonia nitrate are all necessary for the production of explosives and propellants. All of these items can be obtained by the USSR from non-aligned countries, Soviet satellite nations or the West, so it is true to a degree to say that what one free nation may not supply can be obtained elsewhere.

But none of these items belongs to the category of advanced technology, and this is what the Soviet Union wants most: sophisticated electronic products to be incorporated into advanced weapons systems, articles not readily available to them through normal trade channels. Legally, the USSR can acquire what it considers to be essential to the production or enhancement of advanced weapons systems from only a bare handful of advanced countries, and when restrictions tighten they encounter difficulties here. Also the most sophisticated techniques and products are not available through these countries, they have been developed elsewhere.

Disarray in the West over what should or should not be made available to the Russians has been based upon a monumental confusion caused, one suspects, by the fact that nothing like this has ever happened before, certainly not to the extent it has now and perhaps also in an even greater degree by a basic fact of free-world life: unrestricted trade, historically the life's-breath of free societies.

Past policies have embraced a broad view: sell the Russians what they will pay for. Even now, when the evidence of Soviet intransigence is overwhelming and the threat is obvious, this view still prevails, largely because of political reasons and also because underground suppliers can make fortunes without much risk.

It is possible to name a dozen countries conquered by Soviet power since 1949, all of them subjugated by a military machine riding on Western suspension systems, supported by ships, trucks and aircraft built through Western assistance programmes or devastated by weapons systems first developed by Western nations and acquired either legally or illegally by the USSR.

It has rarely been the equipment a nation possessed which determined the path of human relationships: it has been the intentions of its rulers. In a country such as Russia, if these intentions are unrelentingly aggressive and the nation is as dependent as the USSR has been, it can only create the poisonous variety of international atmosphere that presently exists, if other countries make it possible for it to do so.

Nor could the advanced countries have created the Soviet system which now threatens them if they had actively supported any of the export-control organizations established to embargo shipments of Western high technology to the USSR.

There were four basic reasons why support was lacking. 1. The greed of Western businessmen. 2. Government authorities who withheld support for the legal enforcement machinery without which no control organization can function properly. 3. Conspiracies either to destroy the control organizations or to make them powerless. 4. Duplicity to an extent which will be discussed in future chapters.

A control apparatus mentioned previously, the Committee for Economic Development (CED), was only one of several established in the US to monitor Soviet acquisitions. More than thirty years ago the so-called 'Battle Act' and the Export Control Act preceded by one year the creation of an international organization known as COCOM, which was the Paris-based Committee of the Consultative Group of NATO and Japan also known as the Co-ordinating Committee for Multinational Export Controls.*

The purpose of COCOM was to co-ordinate export controls among the industrial nations. Each COCOM member had veto power. Any one of them could have halted the export of Danish marine engines, US machine tools or British technologies to the Soviet Union. Among COCOM members neither unanimous nor majority approval of sanctions is required. Any single COCOM member-nation which considers the transfer of another member-nation's technology or products inimical to its security can halt the transfer by a single veto. If Italian, French and West German direct transfers of military technology had been vetoed by any single COCOM country, Soviet support of Middle Eastern, African and Latin American Communist regimes with advanced weapons systems would not have been possible.

In the US a control enactment called the Export Administration Act expired in 1983. It was replaced by an act sponsored by the Democratic representative from Washington, Don Bonker. The Bonker Bill had a built-in flaw. It was based upon an assumption that US controls would not have to be strong because COCOM, the international control organization, was competent. In fact, no evaluation of COCOM has shown that the organization ever made serious efforts to prevent the export of critical items to the Soviet Union or its satellites among the Eastern bloc nations. Nor has it prevented the re-export of proscribed products from its member-nations to Communist countries.

A study by the Atlantic Institute of Paris uncovered a '... thriving and lucrative business based on surreptitious sales of strategic and military technology to the Soviet Union and Eastern Europe ...' by COCOM members. The Institute's conclusion was that, 'In view of the exceedingly

---

* COCOM members are the United States, the United Kingdom, Belgium, Canada, Denmark, the Federal Republic of Germany, France, Portugal, Greece, Turkey, Norway, Luxembourg, Japan, Italy and the Netherlands.

lax enforcement efforts by certain COCOM countries, the cases that are detected ... may represent only the tip of the iceberg ...'

In effect, COCOM's reason for existing has been eroded by a general acceptance among its members that two specious arguments are valid: 1. that 'non-strategic' items can be safely exported to the Soviet Union, and 2. that what cannot be bought from one nation can be acquired from another. Also, aside from Soviet internal influence on COCOM, there is still a third element. Immense amounts of money are available to brokers and industrialists who are willing to use the Soviet-supported black market for the transfer of proscribed articles. Aside from the millions of dollars which change hands, there is no reason to fear prosecution if caught because COCOM lacks an enforcement capability.

Another control apparatus was the so-called 'Battle Act', more properly 'The Mutual Defence Assistance Control Act', activated in 1951 as a multinational means '... to prevent export from Western countries of strategic items that have the capability of strengthening the military power of the Soviet Union'. Under Section 103(b) of the 'Battle Act' the US cannot give aid to any nation that knowingly allows the transfer to the USSR of strategic items which are listed for embargo by the US State Department. The State Department never used its authority, not even during the Vietnam War when Western nations, including the US, sold military end-products to the Soviets which were sent to North Vietnam.

3

The Unassailable Premise

For years the goal of Western governments has been to prevent the transfer of technology that could be of military value to their enemies, and as a goal it is certainly an unassailable premise, while at the same time and with equal certainty it is a failure.

Forty years after the Kennan Memorandum, Western bureaucrats still managed to maintain a perfect blend of inflexibility and ignorance. In a February 1984 US State Department publication it was stated that, 'It is increasingly difficult to identify and control transactions that could constitute a threat to ... national security because development of sophisticated weapons today depends on many advanced supporting technologies that have dual-use – civilian as well as military.'

The trucks which transported poisonous gas to Afghanistan in 1983 did indeed have a 'dual-use'. They could have served civilian purposes.

The Soviet consumer-goods sector – a case in point the wheeled-vehicle division – was established to provide conveniences. It also had a 'dual-use'. By 1984 the Soviet Union had fifty thousand battle tanks (US: eleven thousand), and fewer automobiles than any single one of the industrialized Western nations.

The 'dual-use' Soviet telecommunications system has provided the military with an abundance of excellent means for monitoring, broadcasting, intercepting and eavesdropping, in a nation with fewer civilian telephones than Japan.

There may be some doubt as to how it can be '... increasingly difficult to identify and control commercial transactions that could constitute a threat ...' when in fact clear and abundant evidence on a worldwide scale offers visible proof that to an authoritarian, military-oriented regime there is no such thing as a 'commercial transaction' which will not be used either directly or through modification so as to constitute a threat.

Although of commercial design, those crawler-submarines used to plot Norwegian and Swedish waters by the Soviet Navy were not engaged in a 'dual-use' commercial enterprise.

The huge automobile factories which were designed, built and equipped by the West in the Soviet Union and for a time were under the supervision of Western technicians, and which produced either no civilian automobiles at all or very few, although created to provide 'dual-use', in fact upon completion began producing tanks, mobile artillery, troop-carriers and supply vehicles.

The identical 'dual-use' variety of tunnel vision in London, Washington, Tokyo, Bonn, Paris, Rome and Copenhagen which created the Soviet war machine, and without which it could not have existed as it does today, continues to influence policies and decisions among the advanced nations. For substantiation see the record of control for embargoed items.

As recently as 1976 a US State Department spokesman said that, 'The Soviet economy is largely self-sufficient. In the 1950s the Soviets built nuclear weapons, sputniks, missiles and nuclear-powered ships without US technology. They could get along quite well without US technology.' That same year all the major industrialized nations encountered increased Soviet espionage and Soviet use of its diplomats to try to acquire articles of advanced Western technology. During the previous fifteen years dozens of Soviet citizens were expelled throughout Europe whose speciality was the illegal acquisition of free-world technology.

The clear fact was that the Soviet Union *could not* '... get along ... without US technology'. Nor could it 'get along' without the technology of France, Britain, West Germany or Japan.

Patently, the tunnel-visionaries were going to endow George Kennan's Memorandum with an enduring relevance

Mr Kennan probably had not envisioned; they still could not distinguish between swords and ploughshares, and as a result, in the areas of embargoes and controls where they exert authority, there have been no certain methods of success but instead vague policies which guarantee only unacceptable risks.

This has been particularly true when profit-motivated business interests use political leverage to sell anything to anyone for a profit, and where organizations such as COCOM share with Simón Bolívar's army the appearance of a large sack with a hole in the bottom.

Reasons to obey the law of the boomerang – or the regulations of control agencies – tend to vaporize before the avarice of entrepreneurs. 'Business,' a newsman once said, 'is the life force of free nations.' He was very nearly accurate. The people who generate wealth in free societies have historically been the movers and the shakers, and the morality which may influence their employees does not appear very often to inhibit the employers.

Commerce and industry own the power in free societies and they do not neglect to exert it in their special interests. But politics is an equal 'life-force', and politics is the vocation of expediency. It is the artifice of being ugly while appearing to be beautiful, of being gifted with a talent for ensuring disasters by convincing constituencies that two inseparables, lying and hypocrisy, are virtues. If the two make common cause, served by tunnel-vision bureaucrats in an era when one set of people can incinerate another set of human beings at ground level, the odds favouring incineration increase very dramatically.

Even politicians of principle imitate the purpose of the cancer cell, which is to encourage malignancy through ambiguity, and perhaps nowhere is this more evident than in Western attempts to stem the haemorrhage of technology or at least accurately and sensibly to define areas where the most critical bleeding is occurring.

No one, excepting those who for their own reasons prefer to say otherwise, can still believe that what the Russians have taken from the West has not been applied to their military superiority, nor that by doing this they have not saved themselves years of research and development (R&D) and millions of roubles.

Even in the free-world the weapons-technology the Soviet Union now possesses could not have evolved in the short length of time Soviet leaders maintain has been the case with Soviet development. An example would be advanced electronic systems free societies pioneered and refined over several decades. Until recently the Soviet Union did not possess a sophisticated R&D scientific capability, and what they did eventually develop the Japanese accomplished in an identical manner fifty years ago: through the establishment of a very large community of very good copyists.

In 1981 a US fisherman netted a bizarre catch, a Soviet sonar buoy. When dismantled by Defence Department technicians, it was discovered that the internal mechanism was able to transmit accurate information to Soviet submarines about sea-water salinity, temperatures and the speed of off-shore currents. But the most interesting discovery was that the electronic chips which performed these functions were exact duplications of circuits manufactured by the US RCA company. They were so alike that they were interchangeable.

What RCA had required years to develop, the Soviets had 'produced' in a fraction of the time without comparable creative talent, sophisticated R&D expertise or equivalent scientific capability. There were three ways the RCA prototype could have reached the Soviet Union. It could have been stolen, it could have been bought, or very likely it fell through the hole at the bottom of COCOM's sack into waiting Soviet hands. The last possibility entailed the least risk, but the problem of controlling West-to-East transfers has a number of built-in failure factors of which COCOM is only one.

Another, probably the least sanguine and therefore the most important, has been the spread of high technology throughout the world with the velocity of bullets. It travelled down along the edge of Asia from the US, fanned out across Western Europe, passed through check-points and cement barriers into Eastern Europe's satellite countries, then down into Latin America, and except for patents and agreements among the nations which pioneered the new-age concept of electronic wizardry, there was nothing that could be done effectively about controlling the spread of it.

A technology-starved Soviet Union certainly had no interest in recognizing free-world patent rights, and there was no reason to expect it to honour agreements either. A US Senate Committee report stated that of '... nearly a thousand treaties and agreements ... which the Soviets entered into with ... countries all over the world ... [they have broken their word] ... to virtually every country'.

Also initial high-tech has been a 'building-block' enterprise. The unsophisticated basics of early experimentation did not require degrees in physics. For years experimenters got by simply by knowing something about radionics; no one had ever made a computer before. The first ones did not have to be complicated. R&D took root from that beginning and flourished, with the advanced nations drawing light-years ahead and everyone embracing the new concept with enthusiasm.

The idea covered the world in a very short time. It was embraced with a whole heart in all lands. There was no way so spontaneous a diffusion could have been controlled. In its simplest variations it offered opportunities for even the semi-talented to plug in, switch over and turn on great varieties of electronic variables. It encouraged ideas as well as experiments.

It was the 'idea' which particularly aggravated the problem of control. In academic and scientific communities where progressive ideas were born, free thought appeared to have vindicated long ago the tradition of free exchange, and both communities were sensitive to, and fiercely opposed, any kind of control.

In 1982 deputy CIA director Bobby Ray Inman wanted US scientists to submit their work for review by Intelligence specialists or face possible confrontation with national security agencies. The result was about what could have been expected from individuals who had been imitating God so long they could not possibly conceive of themselves as Devil's Advocates.

In a similar affair, a 1981 State Department letter to

academies requesting information on research, as well as on the study programmes for foreign science students, raised hackles from the US East Coast to California, the theme of which was unanimous denunciation of '... an intrusion on academic freedom'. An official of the Santa Barbara campus of the University of California said that, 'Basically, what they are asking us to do is apply for an export licence to export ideas.'

Voluntary co-operation was not a success, so the US Commerce Department proposed laws which would make it a felony for researchers to discuss sensitive information privately or in classrooms without obtaining prior permission to do so.

The problems of control in these fields were especially troublesome, for while a tangible bombsight, sophisticated computer or patented RCA electronic circuit assembly was a physical object, ideas were the ectoplasm of pure thought, neither containerized nor visible. They simply did not fit into the categories of things which could be controlled. If they had, much that Eastern bloc countries and the Soviet Union have acquired over the last twenty years would probably never have reached them.

The amount, and the variety, of high-technology ideas in the minds of R&D groups is limitless. Theoretical physicists for example are not limited to open-ended speculations about whether Schrödinger's cat is alive or dead. They can prosper rather handsomely through practical applications of their knowledge to the high-tech scene, simply by rationalizing 'beautiful mathematical formulae' – ideas – into electronic products, and many do. But if they choose instead to spill their guts to Soviet Intelligence, as some have indeed done, what measures could have been taken to prevent it? If no one knows what pure thought is, can a means be devised to control it?

For two years a Russian named Gubin studied the technology of fuel-air explosives under an American professor who was also a consultant to the US Navy. Gubin then returned to Russia. A Hungarian physicist, Georgy Zimmer, was to complete three years of study at the California Institute of Technology. Before his term expired he was expelled from the US as a Soviet agent and returned to Europe with ideas about a particular electronic memory chip the Russians were interested in.

In their original state ideas inhabit a spherical pulsating object the colour of a watermelon streaked with grey which has the texture of jelly. As long as they remain there, as in the cases of Gubin and Zimmer, no airport detection device can identify them as embargoed articles, so the Gubins and Zimmers can smuggle them out of the country without a qualm, and this has been one of the most successful methods of transferring Western technology to the Communist world. The transfer of ideas.

But an idea which travels from the brain to the fingers then onto a piece of paper becomes a tangible item. It can be seen, touched and perhaps controlled. If it appears in published form and violates a regulation, it may very well end up in the hands of a censor. Perhaps the best system among Western nations for the control of published ideas thought to be inimical to national interests is the British 'D-Notice' system, even though its failures have been many and upon occasion quite spectacular.

Other free nations have developed programmes designed to prevent leaks of sensitive information but until recently the US had none. At least it had no official organization of censorship, although in 1982 a bill was proposed to the US House of Representatives which would empower the government to prohibit the publication of anything thought to be a threat to national interests. In effect an American 'D-Notice' system.

But control of published ideas could scarcely be considered as an even poor-to-fair method of keeping Western secrets out of Soviet hands. The flow of technical publications in free societies is enormous. Books, journals, periodicals, brochures, magazine articles appear by the thousands. It has been estimated that Soviet interests subscribe to eighty thousand publications in areas of free-world advanced technology.

At stake in any attempt to control this outpouring of information is a very strong and basic conviction held by free societies: the right of expression – freedom of speech.

It may be reasonable to say in summary that, very simply, free societies have no secrets and that closed societies have nothing but secrets, and that suggestions for controlling ideas in the free-world, during a time when an inundating flood of them is rampant, is absurd at best and at worst impossible to implement.

Nuclear, micro-electronic, chemical and communication technologies arrived in this century with the impact of a soundless explosion, and while the advanced countries have been in the forefront of all this, they have never possessed exclusive prerogatives. Nor are controls likely to meet with much success as long as political and commercial interests close ranks against them.

In 1982 the US wanted a total embargo on equipment required by the Soviet Union to build its 3,600 mile natural gas pipeline from Siberia to Western Europe. The US objection was that if the USSR were able to create a condition of dependency, it could ultimately blackmail dependent nations, increase Soviet control over European energy supplies and finally, through the hard currency gained from the sale of exported gas, materially increase its military build-up.

Europeans, notably the West Germans, had a different perspective. In 1982 they had a 7.3 per cent rate of unemployment, their highest in twenty years. They also had the capital to finance German industrial expansion, and the ability through this expansion to manufacture what the Russians needed and could not manufacture themselves for their pipeline. Further, increased industrial growth would certainly lower the unemployment rate. Nor did they consider dependency as threatening as did the US, perhaps in large part because they had always been dependent on someone for oil and gas.

As for an increased threat from the East, West Germans had been living with that much longer than the Americans had, and while they did not minimize it in their foot-dragging over the proposed US embargo, they seemed of the opinion that a fully employed, thriving national economy, with the threat, was the best alternative to 7.3 per cent unemployment with the threat. Other countries appeared to share this viewpoint. When US embargoes compelled the American General Electric Company to abandon its hope of signing a $175 million contract to supply the Soviets with turbines for their pipeline, an Italian company, Nuovo Pignone, and a British company, Rolls Royce, were ready to bid for the business.

Politically too the pressures against embargoes create problems which have been made to order for their opponents, and generally it is the wealth and power of business interests which influence political decisions.

In the US the Commerce Department, which has a reputation for favouring business interests and which issues export licences, seems to reflect the political ambiguity of succeeding political administrations. In 1980, when President Carter imposed strict controls on exports to the Soviet Union, the Commerce Department reacted unfavourably out of sympathy for US businessmen who claimed Carter's policy enabled foreign competitors to prosper at the expense of US business interests, which was not arguable.

When America's Armco International Company could not honour a contract for generators and turbines for the USSR's Novolipetsk industrial facility, France's Creusot-Loire Company provided them.

The result of business pressure upon governmental agencies whose latitude to disagree with national policies is considerable in free societies weakens the power of administrations that are required to take serious notice of disputes likely to affect political fortunes. In this kind of a climate effective attempts to control the export of 'dual-use' technology can be hamstrung before it starts to move.

When the bureaucratic in-fighting contributes additional dilemmas, both sides, business and politics, suffer. The US Department of Defence (the 'Pentagon') has maintained the position that a pro-business Commerce Department cannot be trusted to proscribe sensitive items. The Treasury Department, whose Customs Service has charge of physically monitoring overseas shipments, has claimed that the Commerce Department, which has a limited field force, does not know what is actually in dockside containers after it issues export licences, and that the inevitable compromise which allows Commerce to grant licences for export, which allows Treasury's Customs Service to prise open crates for physical inspection and which authorizes the Department of Defence to conduct its own reviews and inspections, has resulted in delays for the business community of such lengths that it is not unheard-of for applications to export products in one year being attached to the invoices of shipments which did not arrive at their destination until the following year.

During 1983 the Commerce Department processed 95,000 applications to export. The Pentagon exercised its right of review 2,900 times out of nearly 8,000 instances of shipments to China and the Soviet Union alone, which did not create an insurmountable obstacle to reasonably prompt delivery, but Pentagon authorities wanted to review shipments to friendly nations also, on the grounds that embargoed items sent to those countries were often re-shipped through bloc countries to the Soviet Union. Although this would increase the delay for arrivals, it did not seem to be an unreasonable request inasmuch as it was common knowledge that such trans-shipments did occur.

But the spectre of additional delays, the loss of business this might entail and the bureaucratic bungling and red-tape as well as a broadening of the control this was bound to incur caused associations of businessmen to bring pressure for relief on politicians – if the businessmen were ethical. If they were not ethical, they turned to a well-organized underground export pipeline which required no licences, inspections or reviews and which had excellent reasons to avoid delays.

Prior to the Russian invasion of Afghanistan, Western businessmen did a multi-million dollar annual trade with the East. After the invasion, particularly in the US when then-President Carter imposed sanctions, the agencies which tabulated trade recorded a sharp decline. But actually there were no instances where serious negotiations and sales declined. Nor was this a secret. In a spirit of open rebellion entrepreneurs used the underground pipeline. As a US Commerce Department spokesman said, 'It's business as usual with the USSR.'

As with the overwhelming enthusiasm for the new age of electronics, the equally overwhelming problem of trade-control got nowhere. The unassailable premise still exists. It just does not work.

4

A Confusion of Concepts

According to a general consensus of free-world business communities, no particular prescience is required to understand that choke-off points for sensitive items such as computer-enhancement products will not stop the underground flow of those products from reaching Communist countries, but they will seriously punish businessmen who abide by the arbitrary regulations which in the past have governed such activities. And as far as the US is concerned, where the drain is greatest and where the lead in many, but not all, areas of high technology is undisputed, foreigners who are inclined to favour at least the concept of embargoes have voiced doubts that such a drain could exist without some degree of connivance.

How, for example, could anything as large and critical as the embargoed Digital Equipment VAX 11/782 computer be shipped to Russia through US Customs? The answer is that the VAX 11/782 did not reach the Soviet Union, but it did leave the US (see pages 80 to 85), and that may even reinforce the argument. How could it have left the country, and if anything of this nature can occur in a nation whose outcry is loudest against sensitive items flowing eastward, could it really have been the result of inefficiency or, more likely, the result of something else?

In the decades-long maze of accusations, allegations, charges, counter-charges and investigations which have tended to culminate in scatter-shot obfuscation, whether there was connivance or not, the total concept of control achieved an apogee of unmanageable chaos, primarily because there has never been a method for controlling the control process itself.

In the US the principal legislative act which empowered

the President to control exports, the Export Administration Act, began life as most newborns do, with blurry vision and no teeth. Then the bureaucrats became nannies. A 'Commodity Control List' was compiled, and with the Commerce Department in charge the list grew. When the Department of Defence became part of the review apparatus, the list grew still longer. When the State Department also became part of the process, the long list got longer. Then came the Central Intelligence Agency, the Treasury Department, even 'NASA', the space agency, and the National Bureau of Standards. The list began to resemble the London telephone directory, and the ultimate absurdity inevitably occurred. There were 100,000 proscribed items. One was something which utilized '... analog-to-digital conversion techniques capable of storing transients by sequentially sampling single input signals at successive rates of less than 50 manoseconds'. Whatever it was, it could be assumed that before someone could be found to operate the thing it would be obsolete.

The military compiled its own list, part of which was classified as 'secret' in order to deprive the Russians of information about what they could not acquire from the US on the grounds that not knowing might help them.

Everything is binary, effective in a 'dual-use'. In the years between Presidents Roosevelt and Carter no one appeared to believe wheels functioned beneath anything but cars, prams and hay rakes. After Carter a gradual conviction took root that wheels moved vehicles with guns on them and not much else. Between those years the Soviet Union acquired everything it required to put its armed forces on wheels, and now that that has been accomplished, to everyone's present consternation, anything having to do with wheels, metaphorically speaking, must be on an embargo list.

Presently, several Intelligence agencies have on their proscribed lists a number of 'sensitive' items such as early model computers which the Soviets have possessed for years. Electronic equipment manufactured by the Funac company, the world's largest maker of numerical controls, has long been used to programme Soviet machinery. Japan has been selling sophisticated machine tools to the Soviet

Union for years, the same articles considered as critical in the West. Quite a bit which US list-compilers classify as "sensitive' can be bought over the counter in Tokyo. As a member of COCOM, the Japanese have favoured free trade to the extent that they have avoided use of their right to veto against other COCOM nations in order that other COCOM nations will not retaliate against their own free-wheeling foreign trade. Only recently has the law of the boomerang been translated into Japanese. They are presently aware that their exported technology and the exported technologies of their trading partners have helped the Soviets to develop SS-20 missiles and Backfire bombers. Backfire regiments are being deployed throughout the Far East, directly threatening Japan.

But the free-wheeling continues behind an array of plausible arguments, one of which at least is well founded: not only would it bankrupt a large segment of the free-world's businessmen to comply with the US list of proscribed articles, but to sell the Russians and their client states spare parts for equipment they already possess will not heighten the level of danger very much, if at all, while it certainly would strengthen free-world economies.

Reasoning of this kind is anathema to Western hard-liners, even though complete compliance with total embargoes raises the spectre of economic devastation among advanced nations.

Nor is this dealing in senstitive products always the result of connivance. In many cases it is not illegal. Not all nations have laws against either shipping or trans-shipping critical technology to bloc nations or the USSR. Switzerland does a very profitable trans-shipping business. So do other nations. In fact, if it were not for this legal trade some of the richest dealers in high-tech would not exist at all.

It promotes international exasperation, too, that on some lists of goods not to be sold to the Communists are microwave ovens and pocket calculators. Even though few Russians can afford to buy the ovens, they are available for purchase in the USSR, while pocket calculators are nearly as common in Russia as they are in Britain and France.

An item on one list is aspirin, which brings to mind a remark by the late Nikita Khrushchev to the effect that, if the

West intends to prevent the Soviet Union acquiring 'sensitive' items, then it should add buttons to its list of embargoed products because buttons hold up the pants of Soviet soldiers. Being derisive in this case was perhaps amusing, but in a comparative case it was not. The second case provides a different view of what does not initially appear to be justified.

In early 1980 the US Commerce Department denied eight export-licence applications which, over a period of years, would have provided $1 billion to US companies. One of the embargoed items was yarn. Without an explanation, yarn seems even more innocuous than buttons. This particular yarn was used for ballistic protection and high-strength military structures.

The USSR did not get the yarn or any of the other products on the list, which included computer and research equipment, and speaking as a representative of the manufacturers who had wanted to sell the electronic equipment, an official of the Electronic Industries Association made a remark which has been said so many times it could perhaps be categorized as a Western *miserere*: 'Unless the Administration is successful in obtaining each of our industrialized allies' co-operation in carrying out these sanctions, US efforts to withhold high technology will not work.'

Attempts at co-operation among manufacturing countries have not succeeded. Aside from differing viewpoints on many aspects of what is, or is not, exportable among the free nations and neglecting to consider for the moment the almost limitless compilations of articles someone thinks should not be sold to the Russians or their allies, there is the equivocation factor.

In 1982 President Reagan announced a stringent policy of control on critical products. He said that an agreement with America's allies had been reached which would 'forge an enduring and security-minded economic policy toward the Soviet Union.' To a great many people, if not to all, the Reagan statement was understood to mean that, finally, the Soviets would no longer be able to ride piggyback on Western ingenuity.

That same year, 1982, controls which had been imposed on the export of goods and technology produced abroad by US companies or their subsidiaries were rescinded. Articles which became exportable after the President's announcement which had not previously been available to Communist countries included industrial gasoline turbines, pipeline valves, catalytic crackers for use in oil and gas transmission and refining, analytical instruments, some computers and machine tools.

A further erosion of any policy created to 'forge an enduring and security-minded ... policy toward the Soviet Union' among Western nations was the open door maintained by non-aligned nations. An American company in Connecticut, Perkin-Elmer of Norwalk, received an order for desk-size machines called 'mask-aligners'. They are used in the manufacture of electronic micro-circuitry. The purchasing company was Favang SA, an electronics company in Neuchâtel, Switzerland. Perkin-Elmer applied for the necessary export licences from the Commerce Department. Commerce approved of the sale after being assured by the Swiss government the machines would not be trans-shipped. Favang SA resold the mask-aligners to a Geneva company. From the Geneva company they were sent behind the iron curtain to Prague. The Commerce Department subsequently banned shipments to the brokerage houses involved in the trans-shipments but according to Swiss law no illegality was involved.

In a more straightforward instance an Austrian company which manufactures a sophisticated forge that produces industrial tubing sold its machines to the Soviet Union.

In Russia the big forges were geared to produce gun-barrels for Soviet tanks, including the 41.6 tonne (41-ton) T-72 whose main armament is a 125mm cannon.

According to Ferdinand Lucina, special assistant to former Austrian Chancellor Bruno Kreisky, 'These machines are not especially designed for [producing] military equipment ... It is not possible for a neutral country to say ... we are delivering this machine to the US but we won't deliver it to the Soviet Union.'

Among Europeans, support for the Austrian position is based upon their normal trade, for while US trade with the Soviets and the bloc countries is marginal, European trade with the bloc countries and the Soviet Union is not only a matter of historic intercourse but essential to economic health. According to trade statistics compiled by the International Monetary Fund, Soviet imports, which stood at $7.4 billion in 1974, peaked in 1980 at $21.5 billion. Most of this money went to European companies. Also, according to a 1980 study by the Organization for Economic Co-operation and Development (OECD), the increase in the number of co-operative industrial joint ventures between East and West has been very impressive. Inevitably much of this business, like the Austrian forges, is not only of 'dual-use' but of direct military or military-end use.

In summary, then, Europe, which has historically been dependent on neighbourhood and Russian trade, is in the position of the supplier who must sell to his best customer to remain solvent. If the requirement of his best customer changes from ploughshares to swords, he does not feel responsible even though he suspects the swords will probably be used to harm someone because swords are not of much use for anything else. His business is trade, egalitarianism, economic survival. Unlike the US his home market cannot support him. It rarely has, and the alternative to not trading with Communist countries is unpleasant to contemplate; any list of items the US would like its European allies to join in embargoing, almost limitless in its entirety, simply cannot be acceptable.

What has resulted from this niggling back and forth is strained relations between allies which hurts friends and does not injure the Soviet Union at all.

Even if it were not for such items as the mask-aligners and the Austrian forges, legal articles for export, and the underground pipeline which inundates the Communist bloc with Western technology like water through a broken dike, the Soviet Union would still acquire what it wants through the clandestine operations it runs in all free societies.

Finally, there is a particular US practice which aggravates Europeans and further erodes the prospects for control: US foreign policy.

Acting out of exaggerated concern over human rights or anything at all the US wishes to blow up into a propaganda weapon to make the Soviets look bad, US leaders employ a policy of sanctions without consulting their trading partners, whom they then attempt to pressure into prohibiting sales of items to the USSR which not uncommonly their allies have been selling to Russians for years in over-the-counter transactions.

For Europe and Japan, being caught between the jaws of a US-USSR nutcracker can be an economic nightmare, particularly when US-USSR relations drop into one of their periodic chills within a matter of days. Usually, because there is no advance warning, Japanese and European businessmen are unprepared, and although these periodic and abrupt deteriorations have nothing to do with trade, it is trade which suffers. It is one thing to embargo technology which will enhance Soviet armed power and something quite different to arbitrarily impose sanctions in the furtherance of a unilateral foreign policy which does not coincide with European or Japanese foreign policies.

America's allies are not the only victims of this practice. Under Presidents Carter and Reagan the presidential right to embargo was used a number of times. When Carter invoked it to halt grain sales to the Russians, they bought grain in Europe and Latin America. The net result was that the Russians did not go without bread but the US farm-trade suffered a loss in the neighbourhood of $200 million. When President Reagan embargoed products the Soviets needed for their 3,600-mile gas pipeline, European industrialists took up the slack, the Soviet project continued, and US business lost an estimated $500 million.

Generally, among both Europeans and Americans, when sanctions are clearly desirable there has been an inclination toward co-operation with US policies on export control. But the Europeans at least can do nothing about those devastating little junkets US leaders occasionally take into foreign policy fields and which cause dismay among the entrepreneurs to whom trade means survival.

But American business interests which have been injured and angered can inaugurate action through several channels, including political leverage. The US National Association of Manufacturers, for example, is a large, well-funded, politically powerful organization. It is currently agitating for drastic reforms. Its goal is to see that US presidents are stripped of their power to impose embargoes in the name of foreign policy. The manufacturers believe a president should be required to act through the national Congress for authority to impose sanctions. He should not possess an individual presidential prerogative. It is thought that at the very least US chief executives should be required to consult with knowledgeable specialists on what effect embargoes would have on US and allied business interests before invoking sanctions. There should be consideration on what the economic impacts would be at home and abroad and upon the availability of embargoed items from neutral nations.

A former Deputy Assistant Secretary of Commerce, Arthur T. Downey, has been quoted as saying that presidential sanctions imposed arbitrarily in the name of foreign policy are 'commercial suicide'.

Occasionally something constructive comes out of incipient rebellions. In this case a reasonable and continuing hope remains that presidents, who are successful political survivors, will heed the popular pressure on them to talk tough about Soviet outrages and not do things which injure everyone but the Soviets.

In any case the profession of gamesmanship involving business interests and politics has a long tradition of dimorphic *diminuendo* – the rhetoric of opposing hosts growing fainter with the passing of time and ultimately fading altogether as new, more impelling crises arrive.

That has been the case up to the present time. Councils have convened, conferences have been held, control organizations such as COCOM were born, control enforcement agencies were established, investigative units to certify violations and identify the violators proliferated, and meanwhile the West-to-East technology haemorrhage continued, increased in fact, oiled to perfection by both legal and illegal transfers of a commodity less likely to become obsolete than technology: money.

Nevertheless, in the area of physical efforts conditions have improved. In the US a programme entitled 'Operation

Exodus' was financed through a $20 million transfer of funds from the Department of Defence to the Customs Service. As a grass-roots operation Operation Exodus does not at present suffer from either the divisiveness or the verbal dysentery which prevails on Capitol Hill in Washington. Its purpose is well defined, its personnel are capable, its director, William von Raab, by profession a lawyer, is qualified and sincere. In early 1983 Customs trapped two Americans and a Canadian trying to ship an embargoed diesel-engine assembly line to the Soviet Union using false licences. At New York's Kennedy Airport an Austrian was caught trying to leave the US with an embargoed gun-sight camera used on F-4 military aircraft.

However, while the physical effort at control has improved world-wide, two particular dilemmas remain, and there is a relationship between them.

One, mentioned earlier, concerns the spread of advanced technology. As the profusion proliferates, the power of Western control inexorably diminishes. Recognizing this reality and taking practical steps toward realistic accommodation might result in effective denial of technology to the Russians while simultaneously doing less damage to foreign and domestic business interests.

The second dilemma requires a sound and basic knowledge of what, exactly, the Soviets are after. Technology is a very broad concept. It is also a constantly changing one. The tank suspension and military guidance systems, the micro ball-bearings and other 'dual-use' items required ten years ago – and which the Soviets obtained – are no longer on their shopping lists. In fact, to most people what is of current interest to the Russians, such as that thing '… capable of storing transients by sequentialling sampling input signals at … rates of less than 50 manoseconds', is as alien as Black Holes.

For an even reasonably effective system of control to function, it must be organized around personnel who can recognize what is to be controlled and who can, in a constantly changing scientific environment, stay abreast. They, and everyone else, need a degree of awareness. They require more, the rest of us require less, but even the rest of us have a very large stake in an ambience of war-trek mechanical arts and applied sciences: survival.

5

The Soviet Shopping List

In an affirmation of the obvious US Defence Secretary Caspar Weinberger has said of the Soviet Union that, 'Diplomats and official visitors have been used to ferret out items of interest ... neutral and non-aligned states are targeted for exploitation. Where all else fails, Intelligence missions have been run by the Soviets.'

Without question, whatever method of acquisition is employed, the support organizations are the best in the USSR: the GRU and the KGB. The Western caricature of Soviet agents as bull-necked individuals in ill-fitting off-the-rack suits who hide blueprints in hollow trees and bump into things, if it was ever true, certainly has not been lately. According to a Western Intelligence estimate there are twenty thousand very skilled, talented Russians engaged in obtaining Western high-tech items in categories of which the ten listed below have received priority treatment.

These are the people who illegally bought from Americans sophisticated laser equipment, and obtained through an espionage operation America's advanced TOW anti-tank missile and created two new submarines, the Typhoon attack vessel and the fast, deep-diving Alfa class nuclear-powered submarine, from stolen Western designs. They have also been particularly active in seeking to obtain anti-tank weaponry, radar defence plans, missile guidance and aircraft-carrier specifications. Some of these items have quite likely been acquired within the last two or three years. Others, according to Intelligence sources, have not, but in light of the on-going Soviet effort as well as the very skilled capability of latter-day Russian agents, that may well be an inaccurate judgement.

The following priority items are not necessarily listed in

the Soviet order of desirability but all have been targeted for early acquisition, and according to the CIA preventing them from reaching Moscow 'is one of the most complex and urgent issues facing the free-world'.

1. Soviet submarines, aircraft and missiles have lacked the kind of advanced guidance systems used in the West. There is a great effort currently being expended by the Russians to secure details of Western inertial-guidance systems, as well as electronic and computer devices used for in-flight guidance of aircraft and missiles.

2. The Russians have experienced difficulty mastering solid-propulsion technology. The majority of their ballistic missiles have been powered by liquid fuels. Western missiles use more reliable and safer solid fuels.

3. Soviet inability in the past to develop what Americans call 'smart bombs' has resulted in fair-to-poor Soviet accuracy. They have been unable, for example, to duplicate the superior accuracy of US projectiles which can score direct hits on such targets as moving tanks. In this area, as in others, Russian haste to overtake the West in the quantity of armaments has been accomplished at the expense of quality. But in the matter of tanks, of which the USSR had 50,000 in 1983 and a production level of 2,700 annually (with a ten per cent increase between 1982 and 1983), as opposed to a US tank force of 12,000 vehicles of superior quality, there can be little doubt about the outcome of an armed confrontation.

4. Despite considerable effort by the Soviets to develop a broad system of defence against missile attack, they have not succeeded – at least not very comprehensibly, for while they have the world's only operational ABM system around Moscow to shield civil and military networks of authority, and practically no one else, their reliance is on 'layered defence', i.e. '... defensiveness ... achieved through multiple types of defensive capabilities compensating for shortcomings in individual systems ...'.*

They lack, and need, the varieties of advanced Western technology which can detect the launch of enemy missiles

---

* *Soviet Military Power*, 1984, Washington, DC.

and which can differentiate between decoys and lethal projectiles. A further requirement is the means immediately to process radar information for the launching of defensive antimissiles and invoke a security shield to blanket borders and routes of incoming enemy missiles.

Because Russia's leaders consider strategic defence vital to their comprehensive war plans, their interest in this area is of particular concern.

5. Tsarist Russia built and flew the world's first four-engined bomber a quarter of a century before the US developed one. By 1937 the Soviet Union had the only aircraft capable of non-stop flight between Moscow and the US. It was designed and built by Americans. But since that time Russia has lagged behind the West in two particular areas of aircraft technology. They needed better power plants for their troop and supply air transports which might be required to move men and equipment for great distances, and they were behind in the development of lightweight composites to replace heavier metals in aircraft construction.

6. Aircraft-carriers, of which the Soviet Union had two *Kiev*-class vessels in 1983, are new to the USSR. In 1983 the keel was laid for the first Soviet take-off-and-landing (CTOL) aircraft-carrier at the Nikolayev shipyard.

The US has thirteen large carriers. Between US and British expertise in this area most of the world's experience and development has come to exist through a rather lengthy period of practical use. No one knows more about the construction, maintenance and operation of these great ships. Soviet acquisition of this information would provide the USSR with methods for avoiding expensive errors. It would also halve the R&D time.

7. Also in the nautical area, a Soviet concern has been sophisticated Western anti-submarine technology. The Soviets have lagged behind in this variety of development for years. They were unable to duplicate the kind of listening device Western navies towed behind ships to locate submarines, and no doubt much of this concern over tow-detectors arises from anxiety for the safety of their vast under-sea fleet, presently operating in every ocean.

Many of these vessels, such as the six nuclear-powered

attack submarines launched in 1983, can carry cruise and ballistic missiles.

8. Another problem for Soviet under-sea developers, one which has been concurrent with their haste to build a great navy, has been noise. British and US submarines are quiet. Soviet submarines have been so noisy that Western surveillance equipment has been able to detect their presence even at great distances. In fact, the noise has been so noticeable that it has interfered with their own detection equipment.

The original purpose of Russian submarine designer-builders was to reduce costs, to achieve parity with the US through a crash-construction programme and to achieve great speed in their boats by sacrificing noise-abatement. What they accomplished, while achieving most of these goals, was to make their superior number of noisy submarines vulnerable to detection. They could naturally be expected to seek and acquire Western developments that could overcome this disadvantage.

9. In 1982 a US report stated that in the Soviet Union aircraft' ... designers still bend over drafting boards making detailed drawings of every part of a new plane'. The purpose of this report was to confirm that in computer-assisted design Soviet ability was ten years behind Western designers, who '... routinely use computers to do most of this work'.

At that time the Central Intelligence Agency reported that the Russians were '... clearly impressed by US progress ...' and would most certainly target it for early acquisition.

There is good evidence to indicate that between then and now the CIA, and the free-world in general, had no idea how intense and successful the Soviet effort would be. In fact, in the year it was thought Soviet engineers were still 'bending over drafting boards', the rewards of the USSR's intense underground campaign of illegal acquisition was providing Russian military engineers with a nucleus of technology stolen from Western sources which would make drafting boards almost obsolete. Not, as US exerpts had theorized, by 1994, but by 1984.

There has indeed been a lag in advanced technological

achievements between the Soviet Union and the West, but not as great a one as many believe – particularly not where the application of electronic principles in deployed weapons systems is concerned.*

Largely through theft, Soviet accomplishments in large-scale integrated circuitry and micro-electronics in general have enabled Russian scientists and engineers to duplicate Western radar, lasers and acoustic sensors, along with other detection, signalling and guidance systems more quickly and efficiently and less expensively than ever before, with the result that inaccuracy of weapons can be improved, guidance systems can be calibrated to ideal tolerances, and reaction time, as well as battlefield decisions, can be significantly hastened through the use of high-tech communication systems first developed in the West. And nearly all of this sophisticated information was passing through the underground pipeline while the CIA was writing its report.

It is still passing through. The electronic-assisted products and design techniques under discussion here, which have been targeted for special attention by the USSR, are beginning to appear in both the Soviet civil and military sectors.

10. Finally, and related to the paragraphs above, the Russians especially want Western computer technology and equipment. Everything bearing upon Western computer systems, from plans for making silicon chips to the software instructions that tell computers what to do, are priority items on the Soviet shopping list.

In computer technology, where they have long been hindered by inability to produce satisfactory software and to establish competent fabrication methods, the Soviet drive to acquire Western technology has been and still is intense.

They, and their Eastern European client states, have developed a family of general-purpose, or 'dual-use', computers known as the Ryad series.

Both the Ryad and the Soviet SM series of minicomputers are based on Western designs. They have constituted

* See chapter on Soviet Research and Development.

virtually the total Russian production of general-purpose computers and are used in a wide variety of civilian and military projects. Ryads are copies of the US IBM 360 and 370 series computers which were mass-produced in the US for commercial use and sale. They are readily maintained in the field and are quite versatile but they are not in the same category as the advanced computers presently in use in Japan and the West.

The Soviets are aware of this, and in their drive to keep abreast of more recent and improved computer technology, their major effort to obtain the ultimate in advanced systems has for several years been centred in California's 'Silicon Valley', an area south of San Francisco where several hundred computer companies maintain offices, laboratories and factories. In this relatively small area there are more than four hundred companies engaged in advanced R&D. All four hundred of these companies are involved in classified research, and forty of them are engaged in top-secret projects. In nearby San Francisco the Russians have several buildings – protected by diplomatic immunity – where their best eavesdropping equipment and the technicians to operate it maintain a twenty-four-hour surveillance scan.

Not long ago the degree of importance Soviet authorities attach to this area was indicated when Moscow's Narodny Bank began secret negotiations to acquire three local banks in Silicon Valley. Had Narodny succeeded, the Russians would have known which electronic and computer companies were in financial difficulties, but even more serious, the details concerning personal information on dozens of US scientists engaged in confidential areas of research would unquestionably have reached the KGB.

Certainly, security in Silicon Valley is a matter of great concern – so great in fact that authorities in distant Sacramento, capital of California, very carefully watch every transaction, every shipment, even every hiring practice of Silicon Valley's companies. That was how the secret negotiations to acquire those three banks by Narodny Bank were discovered and scuttled.

But, if there is one fact of contemporary life which has been clearly demonstrated over the past few decades, it is that security shields can be penetrated. If, as in the following instance, the penetration is accomplished by an individual unskilled in penetration, whose motives are entirely personal and who lacks a support-organization to provide documents and training, then it may not be unreasonable to assume that professional penetrators could duplicate his accomplishment and probably have.

In 1977 an application for employment was submitted to the Shugart Company of Silicon Valley, a subsidiary of the Xerox Corporation, by one Mike Noble who had been employed briefly by two other Silicon Valley companies. Noble was cleared by a security check and was hired at a salary of $18,000 a year. He was industrious and likeable and within a relatively short period of time advanced to the position of quality control supervisor at Shugart's San Jośe warehouse facility at a salary of $50,000 a year. He married, became involved in community projects and had been with Shugart, which manufactured computer disc drives, for seven years when he attended a seminar in Santa Clara in 1984. By that time he and his wife, a nurse, had made a deposit on a home.

At the Santa Clara seminar someone thought Noble looked exactly like a man named Walter Lee Parmaran who had escaped from a Virginia prison in 1972.

In early June 1984 two US marshals appeared at the Shugart offices, showed security personnel a twelve-year-old fugitive poster and, when they identified Noble as the man whose likeness was on the dodger, he was arrested, handcuffed and taken away.

Mike Noble was Walter Lee Parmaran. He had been convicted of the 1965 murder of a Washington, DC woman named Shirley Ann Cary and sentenced to twenty years to life imprisonment. The killing had been especially brutal. Shirley Ann Cary's body was found in an alley. She had been strangled, bitten repeatedly and otherwise mutilated so badly that identification could be made only through fingerprints. Her killer, Walter Lee Parmaran, listed as an electronics expert with an IQ of 130, had a long criminal record. After escaping from prison he had established his new identity by viewing microfilms at a public library, finding the obituary notice of an infant named Mike Noble who had died in 1939, then obtaining a birth certificate and driver's licence in the name of Mike Noble.

Walter Lee Parmaran, whose charade was accomplished through an old trick used many times by people in need of new identities, was an escaped felon whose fingerprints were routinely available to anyone making a background check. He was not a trained penetrator, nor could he have been classified as being in the same category as professional KGB or GRU agents. With no professional expertise in deception he managed for over ten years to have free access to all the information the Shugart company possessed. What could he have accomplished had he been a Soviet agent? In 1981 an FBI spokesman said, 'We are blessed with the very best agents the KGB has to offer. They are smooth and very westernized ... We are up against a very professional service.'

Have the Silicon Valley laboratories been infiltrated? Considering the Soviet effort to accomplish this and the ease with which it was done by an amateur, a fair assumption would be that indeed they have been.

There is further evidence not only that Silicon Valley has been penetrated but that the Soviet Union now possesses hundreds of free-world, high technology items it could only have obtained through subterfuge, including such restricted articles as diffusion furnaces, mask-aligners, photo-repeaters, expitaxial growth furnaces, computer-aided design software and much more, all of it under embargo and electronics-related, none of it likely to be the result of indigenous, and less sophisticated, Soviet R&D.

Nor is the spectrum of acquisition limited to the ten listed areas of special concern mentioned above, in which the Soviets have been lagging for years. They have also been deficient in areas of advanced microbiology, lasers and optics, as well as in materials – amorphous, cryogenic, composite, powder metals etc. In Britain, Soviet interest has been keen about significant advances in 'thermal imaging', or night vision. It has also been concerned with the British 'Challenger' tank and the 'Tornado' aircraft.

As shoppers the Russians have a voracious appetite and a somewhat pragmatic, steamroller approach. Although they possess undeniable finesse at the procurement level, their overall strategy appears to function as a juggernaut. When in April of 1983 the French expelled forty-seven Russians for allegedly engaging in high-tech industrial espionage, nothing seemed to change, certainly not the Russian interest in advanced French R&D.

In some ways Western acceptance of the Soviet procurement apparatus is blasé. In 1982 there were sixty Russian inspectors accredited to British factories. In the US the number was greater, but almost impossible to verify because neither the Russians nor US government officials cared to volunteer information.

The procurement technique involves agents who achieve physical contact; the system follows a basic pattern. Whatever the agent obtains is subject to inspection by Russians who are commonly scientific experts. In the US these inspectors function as overseers of routine, legal, Soviet purchases. Whether they are employed by the KGB's department of science and technology or not, everything which is obtained through them is screened by officials of that directorate.

The Soviet Committee for Science and Technology (GKNT), which arranges government-to-government science and technology agreements, establishes standards for legal acquisition. It in effect creates the shopping list. It also allocates the hard currency for payment of legal acquisitions. But it may not have authority to question items which various other Soviet state agencies, including the military, want added to the list. It also passes along the obligation of obtaining embargoed products which it cannot legally purchase but which are on its list, to Soviet Intelligence which then mounts clandestine operations to accomplish the acquisitions.

Some of these Intelligence ventures are relatively simple, if an accomplice can be suborned in, say, Great Britain or the United States. Some are bewilderingly complicated. Many are neither simple nor complicated. For example, it is perfectly legal for an American company to ship high-tech products to West Germany, and while West Germany does not allow direct shipments of proscribed items to the Soviet

Union, there is no law against trans-shipping American high technology to Switzerland, where there are no laws against shipping goods to the Soviet Union (see page 36).

Selling sensitive technology directly to the Soviet Union is a felony in the United States. But selling the same variety of items to companies in Asia, or to foreign brokers in either Europe or Asia, is legal. If there is trouble later, after the equipment has been paid for in Soviet currency and has disappeared beyond Russia's borders, it may be the result of currency violations or tax evasion, but as long as licensing and other requirements have been met, what probably was unethical was not illegal. And there are loopholes.

There was probably never a law which did not sprout loopholes with the abandon of crocuses in springtime. For example, any company within the national boundaries of the United States which has complied with national corporate or other laws can buy the products of any other company in the United States. If, for instance, the purchases are of controlled items, which means they cannot leave the United States, they are still available for purchase by national companies.

Presently in the US there are about twenty companies owned by either the Soviets or the Eastern bloc nations. (Worldwide the number exceeds four hundred companies.) What they seek to purchase is available to them under US law.

Nor has it been necessary to smuggle embargoed prototypes out of the country. Blueprints and specifications can leave the US by way of diplomatic pouches, by the common post or even in a coat pocket.

6

In Search of Success

Operation Exodus, which was initially organized with a $20 million budget from Defence funds, had by 1984 progressed from an uncertain beginning to something rare among government agencies, a dedicated organization less concerned with paper-shuffling than with tough and productive fieldwork.

Currently it employs three hundred special agents and carries out counter-intelligence operations against foreign front-organizations, spies and blackmarket brokers. Within a year and a half of its founding, agency teams had seized over a thousand shipments of contraband worth about $70 million and had secured seventy-five convictions for violations of US laws.

In the new search for success the Americans have responded to the media outcry against the technology drain with belated affirmative action. It is easier for them to do this than it has been for Europeans and Asians. US export trade can be viewed as black and white. Europeans and Asians have been unable to make such clear-cut distinctions.

But three hundred or even twice that many experienced Customs agents cannot possibly plug the dike. While they are watching New York's harbours and airports, the Soviet secret army of at least five thousand specialists operating in the US alone, also in search of success, are achieving some devastating *coups* through other, more distant and porous ports and airfields. In California, for example, recent US breakthroughs in microcomputer technology essential to laser-beam direction a target-selection brought Soviet agents to the office of a small company called Spawr Optical Research, which manufactured especially ground optical mirrors. The Spawr reflector-mirrors direct lasers.

Walter Spawr, owner of Spawr Research, had been selling his mirrors to the US Army for four years. They were vital to national defence, which Walter Spawr knew, and they were directly compatible with military use. In the 1970s Spawr shipped fifty of his precision mirrors to a German contact, who, according to US authorities, re-shipped the mirrors to the USSR with Spawr's knowledge. Walter Spawr was charged with violating US export laws and attempting to conceal the destination of his mirrors. He was convicted of conspiracy and illegal exportation. He offered as a defence his wish to 'help America offset its trade deficit'. According to scientists, this particular acquisition by the Soviets saved them about one hundred man-years of optical research and development.

The Spawr incident was relatively uncomplicated but it emphasized an aspect of illegal acquisition which should eventually be faced: Walter Spawr was convicted for violating the law but the agents who recruited him were not and remain at large to be used again and, presumably, still again.

The bottom line is money. The manufacturers who trade with Soviet or Eastern bloc agents, or with the apolitical smuggler-brokers, rarely appear to be leftists or to share ideological philosophies with Communists. Even more rarely are they motivated by a patriotic urge to help their country redress an unfavourable trade balance. They become part of a conspiracy purely and simply for money.

A particularly damaging example of this was the case of an American engineer named William H. Bell, an electronics project employee of a high-technology defence company. Bell was suborned by an Eastern-bloc Intelligence agent who was vice-president of Polamco Corporation, an export-import company licensed to conduct business in the US under the corporate laws of Illinois and Delaware. Polamco, a subsidiary of the Polish government, engaged in the export and import of tools, machinery and spare parts. It also provided a consultation service for US companies wishing to sell products in Poland. Polamco's vice-president and William Bell were neighbours. As good friends they shared an interest in sports as well as leisure-time activities which included their families.

Bell had financial difficulties. He also had marital problems. Up to this point the suborning followed a time-perfected procedure, one which rarely failed and at which the Soviets were masters. Bell confided in his close friend and neighbour. He also made an effort to impress him by exhibiting classified documents, and from that time forward the leisure-time neighbourhood association moved from the realm of backyard cook-outs to the more hazardous plateau of espionage and intrigue.

At points of rendezvous in the US, Austria and Switzerland, Bell passed microfilm copies of restricted information to Polish Intelligence agents. At one meeting he delivered documents which outlined US and NATO plans for defence against nuclear attack; at another he was given an envelope containing $100 notes. Payment for Bell's services over a three-year period was $110,000.

What he passed to the Polish-Soviet Intelligence connection constituted one of the largest accumulations of secret information to leave the US in years. For the West it amounted to one of the most damaging betrayals since the passing of US nuclear secrets not long after the end of World War II. It included information Soviet Intelligence had been trying to acquire for years. To them it was worth hundreds of millions of roubles worth of R&D time saved. To the West it amounted to a loss of incalculable strategic value, of which the NATO plans for defence against nuclear attack were only one part. Bell also delivered ultra-secret information about the US F-15 look-down-shoot-down radar system, the quiet radar system for Stealth and B1 bombers, an all-weather radar system for tanks, an experimental radar system for the US Navy, specifications for the Phoenix air-to-air missile, the improved Hawk surface-to-air missile, shipboard surveillance radar, a new air-to-air missile and the towed-array submarine sonar system, along with enough additional information about ultra-secret sophisticated weapons-development projects to put '... in jeopardy existing weapons and advanced future weapons systems of the US and its Allies', according to Defence Department experts.

The case of William Bell would not be outstanding except for the hoard of exceptional information he sold. Over the previous ten years there have been hundreds of similar cases, so many in fact it would be impossible to document them all in one book. They certainly emphasize the tragic fact that betrayal has become a day-to-day affair. They also emphasize the incredibly vast collection capability of the Soviet Union, how it operates at the highest, as well as at the most mundane, levels.

For an example of acquisition techniques at the bazaar level, Soviet scientists are regular visitors at science fairs and technology trade exhibitions in Europe, Asia and the Americas, where small companies display fresh technological products and innovative enhancements for use with older systems. The purpose of these visits is so that Soviet scientists can recognize a military-end product and acquire it before home-guard security forces recognize its military adaptability and inaugurate the red-tape procedures which would result in an item being placed under security control and embargo.

This is not a programme which has provided Russia's military-industrial complex with the variety of invaluable information KGB operations have provided, but it is an indication of the scope of Soviet acquisitiveness. Also, every technological discovery began as someone's idea, and emerging ideas have proved vulnerable to well-funded collection efforts.

That look-down-shoot-down radar system used in US F-15 Interceptor Aircraft sold by Walter Bell to Polish Intelligence began life as an idea for putting airborne radar high enough in the sky so that it could look down and identify hostile hardware moving towards a target, without the radar being confused by the earth's jumbled surface in the background. The Russians had the theory but had been unable to reduce a radar system of that complexity to the size of the small box required for installation in aeroplanes. As a result of Bell's activities Russia's Foxbat fighter aircraft now carry the look-down-shoot-down radar system.

Dozens of instances of betrayal are not available for disclosure. Among them may be instances which parallel the Bell case. Other instances are treated as exasperating examples of an immense West-to-East drain the authorities prefer not to think about. Some are allowed to surface to intimidate people who might be tempted or perhaps to encourage a public belief that culprits will be apprehended, possibly also to encourage Soviet respect for the 'due process' inherent in free societies, but penalties for most violators have been discouragingly lenient and almost without exception have punished the wrong people, and it can be doubted that the Soviets have been inspired with respect. The same Polish-Soviet connection which suborned William Bell subsequently recruited another American, James D. Harper, who, for $140,000 over a four-year period sold them the secrets of his country's foremost strategic weapon, the Minuteman inter-continental missile.

Other examples of almost offhand betrayal involve a microchip wafer of the kind used in video games and calculators, the Intel 8224, which has also been used in airborne navigation systems. In 1978 the Soviets mounted a clandestine operation to acquire the Intel 8224. It succeeded. The chip was mass-produced in Russia, then became part of several weapons systems, including the deadly Soviet SA-5 ground-to-air missiles. The Soviet SA-7 heat-seeking, shoulder-fired anti-aircraft missile is a copy of the US Redeye missile. The IL-76 Candid military aeroplane built at the expanding airframe facility in Tashkent in the USSR, is a copy of the US C-141, and the Soviet IL-86 transport is a copy of the wide-bodied Boeing 747. Three hundred of these large transport aircraft were produced in the Soviet Union during 1983.

Occasionally in the past and more frequently at the present time the Soviet search for success has fared poorly, but again, cited instances, while reassuring, probably would be much less so if sealed files in the US, Britain, France and West Germany were available to researchers. Still, recent heightened awareness has prevented some disasters, as in the case of the Adabas computer system, manufactured by Software AG.

Adabas is employed by Intelligence agencies, including the CIA, for analysing secret information. It is also used by armed services such as the US Marine Corps to keep track of supplies, troops and schedules. Adabas is so vital that its codes must be decrypted by a second computer. The people who manufacture Adabas refer to it as 'the Source'.

The Soviets have tried a number of different schemes to acquire a model, or at least Adabas specifications and manuals. Adabas security is very good. A Russian was apprehended in Germany while trying to obtain information about the Source from a Software AG employee. A more sophisticated Soviet agent, Marc de Geyter, a Belgian national, met with Software's president John Maguire at least fifteen times with cash offers for Adabas tapes. Maguire, controlled by the FBI, wore a tape-recorder to many of those meetings. De Geyter's offers increased as Maguire's seeming reluctance continued. Finally, de Geyter approached an FBI agent. That occurred after his offers to Maguire had risen from $150,000 to $450,000. He wanted the undercover FBI agent to steal the Source. He was arrested and brought to trial. His defence rested upon a contention that de Geyter was nothing more than an overly zealous businessman. No proof was available to connect him with the KGB. He pleaded guilty to attempted bribery and received a sentence of four months in jail, an extremely lenient sentence in view of what was at stake – one of the most critical computer systems in the US, the loss of which would undoubtedly have given the Soviets three very valuable keys: one, it would give them the ability to up-grade their armed forces code-breaking ability; two, it would allow them to know instantly the battle-worthiness of troops and supply-support systems; and three, it would not only present them with insight into American advanced computer procedures but also present their R&D organizations with an opportunity to enter a vital US computer system with false, potentially disastrous information.

Partly offsetting this American success is the number of less spectacular but equally critical high-tech items passing through Austria and West Germany, countries with rather lengthy borders with bloc countries. Also, nations such as Sweden who despite professed neutrality in World War II supplied critical material to Nazi Germany up until the last months of the war. Sweden has also supplied Russia with sensitive equipment.

Western Europe has several reasons for engaging in this trade. One, mentioned earlier, has to do with the traditional trade among neighbours without which Europe would slide into economic chaos. Another is the fact that Western Europe's former thirty per cent share of the worldwide electric and electronic market is now only twenty per cent – but with easy access to US technology a respectable amount of the lost revenue can be recovered through clandestine trade – and finally, the decline of Western European ingenuity which at one time dominated many fields, including science, has allowed Japan and the US to overtake and surpass Europeans in nearly all high-tech fields.

Most certainly, advanced high technology, which has been the economic salvation of many countries since the 1970s, did less to create affluence among Europeans than it did among the Japanese and Americans. But the easy accessibility of items which can be re-sold at great profit has made some very wealthy Europeans. In at least one area of high-tech business Europeans dominate: clandestine brokerage. They have developed a degree of finesse more common among international politicians than businessmen.

For example, in California recently two Silicon Valley manufacturers who were concerned over thefts of a great number of their microchips hired detectives to find out who was stealing from them and what the thief was doing with all those chips. The detectives established a 'sting' operation. Posing as thieves with thirty thousand chips to dispose of, they met with a man who offered to buy the chips for 50 cents each. (Their actual wholesale price was $1.50.) The buyer was a Chinese national. When he was arrested, his residence was searched and police found a hoard of advanced electronic high-tech circuitry, most of it with military applications. The Chinese national had been re-selling stolen technology to a US broker who was in turn illegally exporting it to a West German businessman. The West German re-sold directly to purchasers in the Soviet Union. The 'sting' operation was successful but not until after the West German had been providing his Soviet associates with clandestine Western technology for a long time.

These 'sting' operations have undoubtedly been successful because of the Soviet Union's intense programme of
acquisition. But they have also succeeded because
Europeans, and Americans, have learned that the same
degrees of wealth can be achieved through clandestine sales
which were formerly the exclusive prerogative of international narcotics dealers.

Recently the FBI inaugurated its own version of such an
operation. It knew a particular Soviet cruise ship was a
rendezvous for spies. A retired US Navy Lieutenant-
Commander named Arthur Lindberg, formerly a purchasing
officer at Lakehurst, New Jersey, was recruited by the FBI to
go on holiday aboard the Russian ship.

As a passenger Lindberg discreetly volunteered to provide
information to the Russians. He was instructed to await a
telephone call at a public phone booth on a particular New
Jersey highway. The man he talked to had a strong accent.
After being questioned, Lindberg was directed to use the
highway, New Jersey's Garden State Parkway, as his base
for delivering anti-submarine information. The method was
simple: Lindberg would be paid $5,000 for each drop; the
filmed information was to be left at the roadside inside
discarded cartons such as juice-containers.

For nearly a year Lindberg made his drops. Since there
were no complaints, obviously the Russians watched
Lindberg, retrieved his information and were satisfied with
it. They, in turn, were also being watched.

The film Commander Lindberg delivered had all been
carefully chosen by the Navy. Lindberg did not meet his
Soviet associates. Altogether, from everyone's viewpoint,
the operation was a success right up until the day in May
1978 when FBI agents seized a man named Rudolf
Chernayev, whom they had watched recover the material
Lindberg left at roadside, and Valdik Enger, the man with the
pronounced accent who was the telephone contact that gave
Lindberg his instructions.

This kind of clandestine operation is one of the oldest and
least imaginative variety. It is not very clever, and it is
certainly very vulnerable. Nor does it make anyone wealthy.
In fact, to the genuine entrepreneur in search of success,

heavy-handed law-breaking is unappealing because of its inherent failure-factor. Outright illegality will fail. Perhaps not immediately but it will fail.

It does not employ the guarantee sophisticated suppliers of the underground pipeline require: legal opportunities of escape if caught. The same laws which ensure prosecution also provide protection against zealous prosecutors, and loopholes which make the achieving of convictions unlikely; if a conviction is obtained, they automatically guarantee lenient punishment.

If this were not the case, individuals such as an outstanding entrepreneur named Richard Müller would possibly not have been able to operate as successfully for as long as he did.

7

Brokerage

The profit mark-up for smuggling contraband high technology to Soviet and Eastern bloc receivers averages three hundred per cent. In especially critical areas it can go much higher. The limit depends upon what is available and how much demand there is, unless of course an item is a special order, as was the VAX 11/782 computer system, in which case a million or more dollars may be available for purchase.

Inevitably a trade with such a potential for profit has generated a host of brokers willing to feed the underground pipeline which funnels embargoed high technology from the West to the East.

The greatest variety of these items comes from the US, as in the case of the Chinese national working for a US smuggler who re-sold illegally obtained goods to a West German for delivery to the Russians.

The crux of the problem is that, although critical high technology cannot legally leave the United States, it does leave and once it arrives overseas re-shipping it to the Soviet Union in many instances does not violate the law. Nor can US Customs agents do much more than try to persuade European officials to stop re-shipments. Also, since the nations through which re-shipments occur, such as West Germany, will not extradite its citizens for violations of US Customs laws, clandestine brokers achieve success by using the law to protect their trade. They make a point of operating in such countries as Switzerland too, where they are safe from prosecution because their enterprises have legal sanction. They also take advantage of opportunities which encourage exploitation of normal and natural trade. West Germany, for example, has a large technological base which is to a considerable extent responsible for its economic health.

Quite often German companies are licensed as US subsidiaries either to manufacture or to purchase US high-tech items. Otherwise, without a US connection, they can still buy US high-tech products which are compatible with their normal production, and what has legally been acquired in this manner has often been sold to clandestine dealers who provide large profits to sellers and re-ship the items to Russia with little to fear from West German authorities.

Loopholes, many of which are perfectly legal, have enabled some underground dealers to become rich either by invoking laws which protect trade or by devising circuitous methods of obtaining and re-selling embargoed products which are so complicated they are practically impossible to uncover.

One of the most successful of these brokers was Richard Müller, who was born in Berlin shortly after the end of World War II. In the 1970s he was in the United States perfecting a smuggling operation in California's Silicon Valley. He left in 1976 when US authorities trying to plug a high-technology leak identified some of his acquaintances and inspired him to flee. Using a Swiss passport Müller returned to West Germany where US extradition efforts failed because of the German law which blocked extradition for violations of US Customs regulations.

He settled in the suburb of Jesteberg, near Hamburg, established himself as a businessman and began to prosper. After moving to the affluent area of Jesteberg known as Bendestorf, Müller entertained guests from Hungary, Czechoslovakia, East Germany and the Soviet Union. He also developed business contacts in Asia, South Africa and the US. He was director of a number of companies, some legitimate, others front-organizations for his expanding smuggling operation. He could, and did, supply Russia and her client states with a wide assortment of contraband.

Money poured in. West Germany's *Der Spiegel* magazine reported Richard Müller's annual income at $5 million. That he was a genius at organization passes without question.

Quite possibly he was also a genius at bribery, tax evasion, currency manipulation and political manoeuvring. He bought a horse farm in Wiedendorf which had a hundred thoroughbreds, along with the grounds and buildings, and hired a staff to maintain the place. The grounds were patrolled by guards and Doberman attack-dogs and had two assault-proof barbed-wire barriers.

Five years after his abrupt departure from the US, in 1976 Richard Müller was one of the wealthiest independent businessmen in West Germany.

By 1981 the fact that he was a fugitive from US law appeared to have been forgotten in Germany. Nor did German authorities seem inclined to question income tax reports which claimed Müller's German companies had not made taxable profits, although his life-style dazzled other West German millionaires and politicians. He bought the schooner *Tonga*, formerly the property of Monaco's ruling family. He acquired several expensive cars including an exclusive-edition Ferrari.

His Swiss holding company, Dan Control, was immune to outside investigations. He had several close and trusted associates, including a brother-in-law, Harold Bickenback, a Swede by the name of Olof Hakanson, and Volker Nast, who had been identified in 1974 as one of the individuals working with Müller during his technology raids in the US. He also had contacts among other clandestine brokers throughout the world.

It could be safely said of Richard Müller, presently in his forties, that, although near the top in his vocation, he is one among many. The trade he had chosen can make millionaires overnight. Providing aspirants have the abilities Müller obviously possesses, the opportunities are great and the risks are small. Müller is an example, but he is far from being the only example of underground traders who make millions every year they operate.

In 1982 Müller bought a failing company that manufactured musical instruments located between Hamburg on the Baltic Sea and the East German border near Lübeck. The company, Gerland Heimorgelwerke, sold controlling interest to Dan Control for DM 500,000. Müller then changed the company's manufacturing procedures, making Gerland Heimorgelwerke a receiving and trans-shipping organization which handled computer equipment. He particularly wanted products manufactured by the American Digital Equipment Corporation, especially their VAX 11/782 electronic appliance used widely by US military services (see page 38).

In part the conspiracy to acquire Digital Corporation equipment involved Müller and a company employee named Manfred Schröder. To what extent this association influenced Müller's on-going efforts is unclear but Schröder's Digital Corporation connection was fortuitous, for while Müller was transforming Gerland Company into a re-packaging and trans-shipping firm specializing in high-tech products, generally from the US, his effort to obtain a VAX 11/782 continued.

In Russian hands the VAX appliance, which was capable of advanced computations, could enable the Soviet Union to produce sophisticated microchips. It was under intense security control in the US. What it was worth to anyone who could obtain it for the Soviet Union was thought to be between $1 and $2 million.

Müller and his associates made careful plans and meanwhile took advantage of other opportunities to expand their underground trade with the USSR. Re-packaged products at Gerland were falsely labelled, and invoices gave incorrect particulars. A factor which may have influenced the Gerland Company's purchase by Dan Control began to have a bearing on receiving and shipping. Shipments going to West Berlin from West Germany entered East Germany near Helmstedt. Not infrequently they disappeared before reaching West Berlin.

Gerland's thriving contraband trade also used other routes for delivery, and it required a staff to handle receiving, re-crating, invoicing, labelling and delivering. In fact, by Christmas 1982 Gerland and several additional companies acquired by Müller through Dan Control were doing a multi-million dollar export business. Also by that time some Gerland employees whose suspicions had been aroused earlier photocopied invoices showing that a large load of

Digital Corporation equipment loaded at night on a convoy of trucks was going to Soviet and Hungarian state-owned companies.

Müller, who had a residence permit in South Africa and owned a company there, swiftly liquidated Gerland Company and moved to Cape Town. For the second time in six years he demonstrated a knack for anticipating trouble and avoiding it by flight.

His South African company, Microelectronics Research Institute (MRI), which had been established in 1980, was one of six firms held through a holding company, Sem Invest. In turn Sem Invest was controlled by two Swiss firms, Semitronics and Dan Control, both owned by Richard Müller. MRI had its headquarters in a converted shoe factory near Cape Town. It had been obtaining legally exported sensitive US technology for some time before Müller's arrival, reputedly valued at $7.5 million. When Müller and his family reached Cape Town during the last days of December 1982, MRI had acquired the coveted VAX 11/782 computer.

During the course of a subsequent investigation of this acquisition, it was learned through documentation that US Commerce Department enforcement agents had been informed that MRI was a front-company which re-sold US high-tech to the Soviet Union and that they withheld this information from the licensing officials of their own agency and the US Customs Service, which explains how Vax 11/782 mentioned in Chapter 4, on page 34, was able to leave the United States and to arrive in Cape Town.

The US Customs agent who supervised the enquiry into Richard Müller's contraband brokerage business explained the Swiss holding companies succinctly. He said, 'This is a hard-currency game for the Soviets, with their scarce foreign reserves; for their brokers who dislike a paper trail, and for ... US companies which are ready to sell for cash to slightly unusual customers.'

What was not noted at the time was that Müller, who was on the Commerce Department's blacklist, did not appear on MRI's list of executives. MRI was officially headed by a prominent Cape Town management consultant, Dr Atholl

Harrison. It was Dr Harrison's vouched-for respectability by US consular officials at Cape Town which had originally cleared MRI with US authorities so that the company could acquire sensitive computer equipment. According to Dr Harrison, MRI's intention was to organize South Africa's first facility for manufacturing microchips, an enterprise which would establish South Africa among the other electronically advanced nations.

The company established a testing and assembly department. It seems to have been under the supervision and control of three German engineers Richard Müller brought to South Africa. There were also several English-speaking South African engineers. One of the Germans journeyed to the United States for technical courses at Digital Corporation.

Meanwhile additional Digital equipment, some of it second-hand, was received at MRI, where it was assembled and tested. By 1983 when this equipment was operational – perhaps after approval by a Soviet scientist – it was dismantled, crated and shipped to the Soviet Union by way of other Müller companies, some in Germany, others in Sweden.

At this point several seemingly unrelated events occurred. One was the arrest of two South Africans as KGB spies. One of them, Commodore Dieter Gerhart, was second-in-command of the South African Simonstown naval base. Gerhart's wife was his courier between South Africa and Switzerland. At roughly the same time, in November 1983, US Customs officers persuaded Swedish and German officials to halt the shipment of a VAX 11/782 from Cape Town to the Soviet Union.

One month earlier, in October, Richard Müller had very suddenly left South Africa, and although it was claimed that he and Commodore Gerhart were not associates, there was speculation that in fact they may have been.

Seven crates from MRI which reached Europe contained the primary computers of the VAX system. US authorities, who seem to have been operating from secret information passed to them from South Africa, claimed MRI had sold the equipment to a Cape Town forwarding company called Optronix Ltd.

Optronix Ltd was owned by Sem Invest. Optronix re-sold the shipment to a Swiss company which re-sold the shipment to Deutsch Integrated Time. All these concerns were Müller companies. The final destination was a Swedish freighting company owned by Olof Hakanson, Müller's associate of long standing.

Richard Müller dropped from sight but a South African attorney said that no crime had been committed by Müller. What he had been doing, delivering critical electronic equipment to the Soviet Union, evidently violated no South African laws. In fact, throughout Müller's career as a dealer in contraband it was often said that he had not engaged in espionage, which was probably true, but he had not been accused of spying. Eventually he encountered legal difficulties in several countries, but the indictments were for acts which are not commonly considered of great magnitude. His associate Olof Hakanson, an engineer who saw the VAX system's abrupt impounding as US harassment, was critical of US attempts to control re-shipment of US technology in Europe.

Hakanson had been under investigation by US authorities as early as the 1960s for attempting to acquire high technology. In 1981 or 1982 he was involved in a successful raid of restricted high technology by Techmex Company, owned by Richard Müller. Hakanson was not tried because the impounded evidence disappeared from a Swedish warehouse. He was indicted in early 1984 for currency violations arising from his connection with the Müller organization. He was also in trouble over alleged tax evasion.

The contraband computer system was returned to the US but an on-going probe of Müller enterprises suggests that, although the VAX 11/782 did not reach the Soviet Union, other electronic equipment equally as critical did, and may be expected to appear as part of future Soviet weapons systems.

Müller will probably re-surface. That he is on the denial list of the US Commerce Department did not discourage him before; it perhaps will not discourage him in the future. Although Müller's case can be documented by the US Customs Service, as one agent said, how many hundreds of

Müllers are out there? Undoubtedly a great many. Nor are they all so cosmopolitan or as astute as Müller. Neither have they all managed to use the law against itself so expertly. But one fact appears evident: European brokers are superior to the US variety in finesse, possibly because Europeans generally do not look upon the high-tech contraband trade quite as the Americans do.

8

A Plague of Locusts

In 1972 a Canadian attorney of Jewish descent named Peter Virag organized a company called De Vimy Test Lab Ltd. The objective of De Vimy Test Lab was to obtain legally sophisticated US electronic equipment for the purpose of testing and manufacturing computer circuitry. De Vimy Test Lab was allegedly on the outskirts of Montreal and, because Canada was classified by US authorities as a 'friendly nation', De Vimy company was able to buy classified equipment of strategic value, which was not to leave Canada.

After several years of doing business with US electronic companies, it was learned that there was no De Vimy company. What was sent to De Vimy was delivered to a Customs broker near the Montreal airport, where it was sent to Amsterdam. From Holland it went behind the Iron Curtain. A considerable amount of the De Vimy purchases had been designed to manufacture semi-conductor chips of sophisticated design.

When Peter Virag was interrogated and during the course of the questioning mentioned a 'Jacob Kelmer', investigators suspected that what they faced was not simply another instance of an unscrupulous businessman but an international clandestine operation. They knew that Jacob Kelmer was president of a Haifa company known as Excel Industries and that he recruited suppliers of high technology through front-companies where his name did not appear. Kelmer had a master's degree in electrical engineering from the Rennselaer Polytechnic Institute of New York and although he had been born in Israel had also lived in the United States.

As early as 1970–1 it was known to US authorities that Kelmer had acquired restricted US high-tech items including

71

advanced oscilloscopes capable of functioning in broad band-widths or at extremely high frequencies, which were necessary in the testing and maintenance of nuclear weapons, telecommunications and lasers. At that time – 1972 – Kelmer had indicated that none of this equipment would leave another 'friendly' nation, Israel. But it did leave, if it ever arrived there. It was traced to Austria, then disappeared, and Jacob Kelmer was placed on the US blacklist; he could no longer buy US high-tech items.

According to Peter Virag, Kelmer said he was an Israel army officer and that Israel needed advanced electronic systems for defence. Virag, it turned out, was not an independent businessman: he was Jacob Kelmer's employee.

According to a news release in the late summer of 1980, Kelmer told Israeli investigators that he told Virag what to purchase. He also told Virag that when clandestine shipments reached Amsterdam, he re-shipped them to East Berlin, Prague and Warsaw. Kelmer organized the De Vimy Test Lab cover with Peter Virag as executive-in-charge, and although it was said that he had visited Canada, he did not do so often, nor did he stay long when he visited.

The year following De Vimy's founding Virag acquired a number of US electronic products of strategic value but which were not considered highly sensitive. Then De Vimy was able to buy a chemical reaction chamber for use in producing gallium arsenide, an element of the light-emitting diodes in computer systems which was of vital importance in microwave communications. De Vimy immediately shipped this appliance to Holland, where it was re-freighted to East Berlin, and when the US company which had sold the system to Virag reported to the Commerce Department that their appliance had left Canada in violation of the terms of sale, an investigation was undertaken.

Meanwhile, Kelmer told Virag to obtain the specifications of a US-manufactured photo-repeater. This system etched integrated circuits onto semi-conductor chips.

When Virag obtained the photo-repeater information and forwarded it to Kelmer at Haifa, orders came back for Virag to purchase one of the units manufactured by the GCA Corporation of Bedford, Massachusetts. The GCA photo-repeater was far advanced over anything like it possessed by the Russians. Virag arranged for the purchase with funds from an account in a Canadian bank which was regularly supplied with money from Switzerland, and GCA Corporation arranged for the shipment to Montreal from Massachusetts by truck.

The day after the shipment reached Montreal, it was sent to Amsterdam. By the time investigators traced the shipment in Holland, it had already been sent to Prague, where presumably it began its final journey to the Soviet Union. Jacob Kelmer, who had been placed on the US denial list in 1971, was still doing business in 1972, and on up to 1980.

Both Peter Virag and Jacob Kelmer were indicted by a New York grand jury, but although a warrant of arrest was issued for Kelmer, he had little to fear providing he did not return to the US because his latest offence was not covered by extradition treaties. This time he was put on the blacklist for fifteen years, something which did not mean much to such enterprising businessmen as Jacob Kelmer or Richard Müller. As long as they could find willing individuals to buy for them and equally willing companies with products to sell, and as long as they could protect themselves by using the law to do it, there was very little inducement for them not to supply the Soviet underground pipeline and make fortunes while doing it.

It is interesting to note that Soviet satellites for military use which parallel US development in the higher frequency fields became operational in the 1970s, about the time Müller and Kelmer were sending great amounts of Western high-tech to Russia. The Soviet Raduga ('Rainbow') geosynchronous orbit satellites, for example, operate on the same 8/7-Ghz band used by the US Defence Satellite Communication System's DSCS-2 spacecraft.

Two interesting sidelights of the Virag-Kelmer affair which surfaced during the investigation of De Vimy Test Lab Ltd concerned the De Vimy bank account in Montreal and Jacob Kelmer's orders to Virag. All questions about the bank account stopped in Switzerland but Kelmer did not appear to be the source of the money which was transferred to Canada. Also, Kelmer, like Peter Virag, was an employee;

that trail led to London but by the time investigators got that far, whoever it had been who told Kelmer what to buy had disappeared.

Presumably the London contact was part of a very extensive Soviet European ring. The year before De Vimy was organized in Canada, a Soviet attempt to acquire high technology in Britain resulted in an unprecedented expulsion of Russians: 105 were ordered to leave the country. According to the London *Times* (25 September 1971), they had been engaged in military and industrial espionage. Specifically, they had been seeking to obtain information about '... electronics, transformers, semi-conductors, computer circuitry and technical details of the Concorde and Olympus 593 engines'.

A probable connection existed between Soviet agents in Britain and Russian industrial procurers operating in France. Using diplomatic cover, the Soviet ring in France was interested in the French aircraft company Aerospatiale, the aircraft engine-manufacturing company, Snecma and the European Airbus 310. Nor did the conspiracy end there. The French counter-espionage bureau, *Direction de la Surveillance du Territoire* (DST), exposed a conspiracy among Soviets under diplomatic cover to obtain the specifications of Air France's aero-control system.

In April 1983 French authorities expelled forty-seven Soviet citizens who were allegedly seeking to acquire French high-technology items. Several of the Russians were diplomats, the remainder were commercial attachés, but like a plague of locusts, for each one the Western nations rid themselves of there was no end of replacements.

In France long-haul trucks from Bulgaria which were equipped with electronic detection systems and sophisticated cameras developed for covert work used routes which took them past French high-technology installations. In Sweden vehicles with diplomatic licence plates did the same but with an additional advantage: the vehicle roofs had been treated with a special compound which allowed Soviet satellites to monitor their movements. In this way the Russians were able to determine precisely where Sweden's high-technology as well as military installations were located.

This kind of espionage was not discovered in Sweden for a long time and, presuming that it proved satisfactory for the Russians, there appears to be no reason to believe it had not been used elsewhere and conceivably is still being used. But locating high-technology facilities rarely requires such strenuous effort. A recent East German defector brought with him some enlightening material. One West German electronics company out of dozens had approximately forty employees who were delivering secret information to the East Germans.

There is abundant evidence that West Germany is perhaps the most thoroughly penetrated country in the West. Certainly its proximity to East Germany makes this possible. Also, weak enforcement of export regulations, easy access for brokers in need of sanctuary, and a general lack of knowledge among businessmen about how to cope with the horde of procurers in their employ, make the transfer of Western high-technology to the Soviets through East Germany very easy.

For German businessmen engaged in legitimate enterprises, it amounts to an intolerable situation. When sensitive high-tech items controlled by US patents which are manufactured in West Germany with US permission turn up in Soviet possession, US authorities quite often threaten to cancel agreements which allow the West Germans to produce the items. To the Americans protestations of good faith have not been enough, and in justification of their stand it has been cited that the Soviet Union's main provider of Western industrial secrets has been East Germany.

Out of desperation a consortium of West Germans undertook the support of an establishment called the School for Economic and Industrial Security, located near the town of Bad Oldesloe in northern Germany in a large, functional, rather unattractive building atop an isolated hill.

The School for Economic and Industrial Security (SEIS) is the only institute in Western Europe where industrial counterspies are trained on a professional and full-time basis. It was created largely to counter East German industrial pirating. SEIS is operated by the DSW Group, a security organization which not only trains agents in methods of detecting and apprehending industrial thieves but also provides bodyguards, electronic surveillance and general private police services. Most of SEIS's personnel have been drawn from the West German border constabulary or the army, either non-commissioned officers or junior officers with up to twelve years of service. The remainder of the enrollees come directly from industry. Instruction is by a revolving staff of qualified professionals from a variety of security fields, and a number of European and US companies have been SEIS clients, including Hewlett-Packard of California and Citibank of New York.

SEIS was founded in 1979 by a former brigadier in the German army but in 1981 a businessman named Siegfried Neubert became manager. Neubert improved the curriculum, broadened the base of instruction and improved the SEIS profile. It now has a waiting list for admission.

SEIS has had results. It is an outstanding organization. Its counter-espionage course accommodates forty enrollees, the same number as were stealing high-tech secrets from the one West German company mentioned on page 95.

As one of Western Europe's most productive societies which is engaged in the development and production of high-technology, West Germany has a great number of high-tech factories. Forty skilled counter-intelligence agents could quite possibly be four hundred and still fall short of the optimum prevention requirement.

Policing, while desirable, appears as only part of a manifold solution. Nor does it seem reasonable to expect even a very good industrial counter-intelligence organization to possess the capacity to stalemate a huge, well-funded, massively manned state agency such as the Soviet KGB, which now has as its chief focus the acquisition of free world high-technology.

Even were West Germany's School for Economic and Industrial Security incorporated into the US Exodus operation, the number of operatives would not approach one thousand. By Intelligence estimates there are five times that number of Soviet spies in the US alone.

The scope of blackmarketing exceeds the ability of most policing organizations to prevent it, for while uncovering individuals such as Virag and Kelmer who operate at the procurement level, there are others operating at an executive level who are not as susceptible to routine exposure, and there are a great many of them.

In Sunnyvale, California, I.I. Industries shipped proscribed microcomputer systems to a West German company labelled as 'air-conditioners'. From Germany the shipment was sent through Switzerland to the Soviet Union. The I.I. Industries shippers were three company executives who were ultimately apprehended and indicted, but the point is that security guards would not be in a position to oversee the activities of a company's chief executives.

Soviet agents, thieves and blackmarket brokers are only part of a problem which includes business executives willing to funnel restricted technology through the underground pipeline, and it is more difficult to uncover them than it is to uncover ordinary violators.

The matter of falsifying applications for export licences and the invoices which accompany illegal shipments invites some risk of detection, but that amounts to a calculated hazard in a very lucrative trade. In the United States 75,000 export licences were granted in 1980 and 1981. Between August 1980 and May 1981, ten months, US Customs officials stated that unauthorized shipments of high-technology worth $8.3 million were seized in Los Angeles; by using some arcane formula it was then assumed that at least twice that much got out of the country nationwide. Much of this hoard was uncovered through tips and routine spot-checking. All of it was mislabelled with the obvious intention of deceiving US authorities, and although no substantiating statistics are available, there can be little doubt that many of those shipments were sent on their way with the knowledge of company executives.

But there is a related drain of Western technology which does not leave Europe or the US in large crates. It flows from the West to the East by diplomatic pouch, by ordinary letter or in a coat pocket. It consists of secret formulas which have been developed on a small scale in Western experimental laboratories. It involves immobilizing chemical and biological weapons (CBWs), and the formulas which have reached the Soviet Union have been studied, improved upon and produced in great quantities for military use.

At the present time the USSR has the largest stockpile of CBWs in the world. Over a period of twenty years, more particularly during the last ten years, the Soviet CBW programme has surpassed the free world in the development of both chemical and biological weapons. A particular difficulty in perfecting these weapons has been testing them. Prior to being committed for use they must possess stability, adaptability to delivery methods, and lethal persistence. In other words they must not be neutralized by atmospheric conditions, their deadlines must persist after delivery, and they have to be deliverable by low-flying aircraft over wide areas without being either diluted or dissipated during delivery.

Afghanistan provided an excellent area for testing CBWs, and they met the requirements admirably. A particularly rapid incapacitant known by Afghans as 'the silent killer' flash-killed victims in seconds. The West has nothing to equal this agent for ground use.

Among biological warfare weapons currently being studied in the USSR are biologically active silicon-containing and organofluorine compounds as well as marine neurotoxins including blue-green algal neurotoxins, enhanced sleep-inducing peptides to paralyse neuro-motor systems, and improvements on the 'yellow rain' compounds which have been credited with having killed thousands of people in south-east Asia, and identifiable as the cause of death by a unique characteristic: victims' ears turn blue.

As a result of a Soviet Central Committee agreement to authorize and fund CBW research and production, in violation of the 1971 Biological Weapons Convention against such R&D which the Soviets signed, eight R&D facilities were established under the Defence Ministry's Seventh Main Directorate. Two particular centres are at Zagorsk and Sverdlovsk. The Zagorsk facility operates under a cover name: 'The Scientific Research Institute of Sanitation'. At Zagorsk there are high security special storage areas capable of containing enough biological warfare supplies to devastate Europe. An older research, production and storage facility is at Berdsk in Siberia, adjacent to the US. The Berdsk installation was enlarged in 1984. All three of these facilities plus an additional six use front organizations which engage in pharmaceutical, agricultural and medical research.

There are CBW storage facilities in the USSR's satellite states with hard evidence that in the event of a conventional-style conflict they will be used against Europe. Also, in Matanzas province, Cuba, Soviet instructors have been training Cubans at a special forces training centre at Linomar in the use of CBWs with emphasis on US targets. There are CBW storage installations in Cuba so sensitive that most Cuban officers are not allowed access to them, and the largest of these installations is guarded by ground-to-air missiles.

Over the last ten years Soviet CBW technology has achieved a sophistication superior to anything like it in the free world. The US National Security Council and the Central Intelligence Agency have information concerning these Soviet advances which the scientific community considered impossible just ten years ago. Nor is Soviet development of unorthodox warfare techniques limited to CBW weapons. Soviet scientists have mastered biotechnological gene-splicing techniques that can destroy entire populations. In terms of human survival, gene-splicing is as ominous as the atom-splitting discoveries which led to the nuclear bomb.

The idea that the Soviets would not use these weapons is contradicted by the fact that they have used them. Further, the deadlines of their experimental cultures was demonstrated when the on-going R&D at Sverdlovsk created a particularly deadly strain of anthrax that killed hundreds of Russians in April 1979 when a small amount of the BW agent got out of control.

In 1982 the Soviet Union signed another agreement which was drafted by the International Biological Weapons Convention that prohibited the manufacture of such weapons, but unfortunately the history of Soviet signatures on treaties is not encouraging. As early as 1919 a prominent Communist – they were called 'Bolsheviks' then – said, 'We are willing to sign ... anything ... it would only mean we should put no trust whatever in the piece of paper we should sign. We should use the breathing space so obtained in order to gather our strength.' Moving ahead more than a generation, Josef Stalin said, 'Words are one thing, actions another. Good words are a mask for the concealment of bad deeds.'

There is indeed evidence that the 'good words' have concealed the 'bad deeds'. Despite having signed anti-biological treaties, the Soviets have produced and used and presently have in storage more of this kind of deadly biotechnology than all the other nations in the world combined.

'Gene-splicing' is defined by a number of different names: 'recombitant DNA technology', 'genetic engineering', 'synthetic biology' and 'biotechnology', but whatever the designation it is the study of DNA, deoxyribonucleic acid, which is the basic genetic ingredient. Soviet scientists have mastered the process of removing bits of DNA from the cell of one species and grafting them to that of another, which in effect creates a new organism.

Potentially, what this means in military terms is frightening. New substances could be created including enhanced viruses which would be many times more deadly than anything before encountered by life on earth and against which present anti-virus drugs would be useless. It also means brain-eroding agents could be put into projectiles which, when they reached a destination, would emit a fog. Such bio-gas would destroy animal brains, two-legged as well as four-legged.

The aftermath of this kind of attack would be worse than the results of the atomic bombs used against Japan in World War II. It would be an efficient and inexpensive way to destroy millions of human beings, crops and wildlife. It would certainly make some varieties of domestic animals extinct. Its implications are so nightmarish that scientists have chosen to believe no such R&D is being conducted in the Soviet Union.

The evidence points in a different direction. A CIA report states that 'sporadic ... allegations have been received concerning Soviet involvement in offensive biological weapons development. Sources of the allegations have ranged from low-level defectors to high-level Soviet academicians'. The same report notes further that developments have been monitored by several (European) Intelligence communities and that as a result it has become known that the USSR has acquired 'significant technology and equipment, built large-scale biological and fermentation facilities, and made progress in other areas ...' whose purpose is the production of weapons for use in biological warfare.

There are those who question the Soviet capability and those who deny it exists. The US fits into neither category. Its Department of Defence budget for biological warfare research has increased fifty-four per cent since 1980.

A number of Europeans have raised the question of just how qualified *is* Soviet research and development. If it is actually as unsophisticated as has been claimed over the years, then with respect to chemical and biological warfare, possibly someone's irresponsible hysteria may be at fault for raising the spectre of a depopulated world.

If it *is* as sophisticated, then that fact should be authoritatively established.

9
R&D

Perhaps in part because for twenty years Western authorities have maintained that the Soviet Union has been unable to match the free-world in research and development, and also because it has been to the USSR's advantage to encourage that belief, it is still thought to be true in the 1980s.

To some extent there is a gap but it is not as wide as is generally assumed and in some areas the Soviet Union has not only achieved equality but taken the lead.

Soviet R&D programmes are extensive and thorough. In 1984 there were 3,200 research institutes engaged in scientific and technical (S&T) research, nearly all of which were military oriented, and over the last decade parity with the West has been achieved in nearly all scientific and technical provinces.

Nor can it be claimed with truth that this is entirely the result of legal and illegal acquisitions of free-world advances, for although they have certainly provided the Soviet Union with prototypes and guidelines without which Russian R&D could not have closed the technology gap so quickly, underestimating the brilliance of Soviet scientists is a mistake. They have demonstrated many times that, given the technical data, they can improve upon it and that they are creative on their own initiative. An example would be an efficient electrical power source for mobile laser weapons, an area in which the West has not produced anything equal to the Russian rocket-driven magneto-hydrodynamic generator capable of producing fifteen megawatts of short-term electrical power for laser weapons in areas, or under conditions, where normal electrical power would not be available.

The major thrust of Soviet S&T research has been in the development of space systems, missiles and military aircraft.

In this region the growth rate over the past decade was thirty per cent. For high-priority aerospace programmes it was higher. For example, the Tupolev Design Bureau, which was responsbile for the new Soviet strategic Backfire bomber, has doubled in size over the last decade, while agencies responsible for naval and ground-forces offensive and defensive weapon systems have done nearly as well.

Russia's military-oriented national leadership has allocated R&D the highest priority despite a rather general decline of the Soviet economy over the past six years, and this has increased the worry in free-world chancelleries that Russia's leaders may be pushing toward a war-making deadline. The growth rate of capital investment in military development has been increasing at a rate of approximately seven per cent a year while the national economy has slowed to near stagnation level. Further, the intransigent attitude among Soviet leaders, dominated by the military sector, has encouraged a wider and more distinct separation between the military and civil areas at the expense of the civil. It has also aroused concern outside the Soviet Union that earlier Russian zeal for spreading Communism throughout the world has been replaced by a military ideology which uses the earlier Soviet motivation as an excuse to create a purely military system whose objective is the spread not of Communism but of armed conquest.

Toward this possible objective, and in recognition that future conquests will depend greatly upon sophisticated weaponry, the Soviet leadership has also expanded its S&T facilities. Presently the USSR graduates 500,000 scientists and engineers annually.* Russia has the largest number of research and development specialists in the world: 900,000. The best of these are assigned to military R&D, and although individual initiative in a rigidly controlled society is not desirable, and this lack has certainly impaired Russian innovativeness, where it has been allowed, as in duplicating and improving upon acquired free-world technology, Soviet scientists and engineers have demonstrated competence.

* In comparison the US graduates 100,000.

A fact which supports the belief that war-making is now the Soviet Union's objective can be found in the tenure of officials who, as politicial, scientific and industrial leaders, have charge of R&D and S&T as well as the national economy. The late Minister of Defence Dmitry F. Ustinov, who survived purges, replacement and falls from favour, was an excellent example. For more than a quarter of a century during internal political upheavals and several bloody purges he not only survived, he steadily advanced until he became a member of the nation's leading councils including the Politburo. Ustinov, like all top Soviet military leaders, demonstrated over many years that his exclusive concern was Soviet military superiority, the ability to wage war and the willingness to do so.

As in Ustinov's case all Soviet supreme executives have been and are either directly associated with the military or, are subordinate to it in their official capacities in the research, development, scientific and technical sectors, fields which have become quite large, efficient and productive. They have followed a time-tested sequence: the development of weapons systems and the enhancement of acquired systems are subject to scrutiny by the Soviet Academy of Science and the several ministries of defence for military-industrial production as well as a number of design bureaus where development and enhancement programmes culminate in construction of prototypes. From the design bureau workable and presumably satisfactory systems are sent to manufacturing factories.

At the top of this process is the Ministry of Defence, where weapons requirements originate. Next come the approval of the Chief Party Authority – presently Mikail Gorbachev – and authorization for funding. Because military funding has top priority once the Ministry of Defence has originated a requirement, what follows is routine. Also, because approval at the Politburo level carries the force of law, if there are doubts they do not surface. And it is incumbent upon those upon whom responsibility falls to make haste.

If this procedure seems complicated enough to ensure delay, it is not. Basically it amounts to Defence's request being implemented from top to bottom unhampered by Parliamentary or Congressional debate. It cuts to a minimum the time between stating the need and producing the weapon. If this were not so, the USSR would have been unable to achieve parity with the West, and in some cases superiority, in ten years, to produce the most formidable war machine ever, and the greatest progress has been since 1979, when the Soviet economy began to stagnate. Between 1979 and 1983 the USSR produced 160 bomber aircraft. (NATO produced none.) During the same time span the Soviet Union produced 6,000 fighter/fighter-bomber aircraft. (NATO produced 675.) In the missile field, where R&D and production have escalated noticeably, the USSR produced 1,600 ICBMs. (NATO produced none.) The USSR produced 26,700 SAMs. (NATO produced 6,000.) The USSR produced 55 submarines. (NATO produced eight.) The Soviets produced 99 major combatant warships. (NATO produced 25.)

Obviously Soviet Military planners not only are able to order and sustain the resources necessary for the production of desired weaponry but can do it faster and more efficiently than any Western nation can, and it is this ability, plus their significantly increased good fortune at acquiring Western technology, which has helped them greatly in another area: time. The time saved is not limited to the uniqueness of their political and social system; it extends to their R&D process.

Each acquired high-tech system is the product of someone else's lengthy development and funding, and that makes a great difference. What Western European or US scientists may have spent years perfecting and millions of dollars to produce arrives in the Soviet Union available for whatever modifications are required in order for the system to be incorporated into a Soviet military weapons system without delay. Nor for a long time has it been Soviet practice to obtain Western technology on a hit-and-miss basis. Planners have in cases of record started production of weapons which could not be completed until some particular advanced item was obtained in the West, which implies a rare degree of confidence in their acquisition techniques.

It has narrowed the gap between the USSR and the

free-world. It has also altered the thrust of their Intelligence policy, which in former times was almost exclusively concerned with foreign political and military affairs. It is now and has been for the last decade or so involved in abetting thefts of Western high-tech. If Western Intelligence estimates are reliable in this respect, there are thousands more Soviet agents engaged in the acquisition of sophisticated Western high technology now than there ever were tiptoeing along the back stairs of Western chancelleries seeking the political and military secrets of other nations, and what this almost obsessive singleness of purpose has accomplished poses a threat which cannot be underestimated.

Soviet weapons, which were formerly not noted for accuracy or sophistication because they lacked comparable electronic enhancements to ensure these characteristics, have benefited greatly from recent acquisitions. Advances in large-scale integrated circuits along with other microelectronics have enabled the Russians to utilize acoustic sensors, advanced radar, laser and pin-point guidance systems which they could not have developed through their indigenous R&D except over a longer period of time than was required elsewhere. But, given prototypes, they have been able to make state-of-the-art copies, very often with significant improvements.

Also, until recently, because they were not adequately proficient in computer technology, their weapons systems did not compare favourably with US and European armament. Then the Soviet R&D and S&T infrastructures were reorganized so that a great part of each was no longer engaged exclusively in indigenous research but geared to await the arrival of free-world technology which was copied and quite often improved upon. In effect, Soviet R&D made a quantum leap from crawling to running.

Their ability to innovate from someone else's discoveries has enabled Soviet scientists to carry acquired knowledge to great lengths. Their progress in computer technologies, for example, in which they were deficient for so long, has not only resulted in very progressive manufacturing advances but also put them in the forefront of robotics and artificial intelligence research, both of which possess a very definite potential for military use, particularly in unmanned attack systems which would be immune to such things as radiation, shock or the requirements human beings cannot do without, such as sustenance. They would also be invulnerable to death although not invulnerable to destructive heavy projectiles, but even then they would be salvageable.

In what amounts to the heart of their military effort, manufacturing, they have made great strides. Beginning in the euphoric days following the First World War, Western nations went to great lengths to industrialize Russia. They continued doing so until fairly recently, and the result has been that, given the initial turnkey factories, the training and guidance provided by France, Italy, Germany, the US and Great Britain, Soviet engineers have matched Western manufacturing advances. They no longer require assistance in this area. In fact, Soviet heavy industry can out-produce most Western nations and not only in the production of armaments, although that is what it has been engaged in for the last twenty years.

Where the Soviet manufacturing system has lagged is not in fact the fault of the manufacturing process. In the West great advances have been achieved in the perfection of materials of military significance including steel, advanced composites, titanium alloys, super-alloys and aluminium alloys. Because much of this knowledge was not available to Soviet factories, their production was limited to what advanced foreigners had considered adequate a decade earlier: casting, forging, welding, metal extrusion, the accepted procedures for working traditional metals.

The manufacturing process was excellent. Otherwise, obviously, it would have been impossible for the Soviet Union to have produced so much so fast.

The process was inevitably slowed when Soviet R&D eventually introduced sophisticated materials for which considerable re-education was required. But those who saw in this drop of production some variety of attrition – the deterioration of machinery, the incompetence of managers, a lack of worker incentives or the incompetence of a social system which made a mess of the national agriculture – saw what they wanted to see, not what they should have seen.

With some reorganizing but mostly re-educating, Soviet factories, having benefited from national R&D programmes, made a transition from traditional to advanced procedures. As a result of strong encouragement they now apply advanced fibre-reinforced composites to military systems with as little difficulty as they processed heavy metals a few years ago.

The advantageous ratio of strength to weight of new metal alloys and polymeric materials has been recognized at the manufacturing level and absorbed into current manufacturing procedures. These innovations, along with ceramic-based enhancements and high-performance carbon, have to some extent replaced older, more traditional materials in the production of missiles and aeroframes. Titanium, for example, has taken the place of less resistant traditional metals used in submarines. Fresh techniques of manufacturing had to be developed, and they were, essentially because the Soviet manufacturing sector learns quickly, works efficiently and possesses the plants, tooling and skilled manpower to accommodate change.

In summary, the strongly military-oriented Soviet manufacturing sphere, which is where all the designing and planning end and without which there would be no Soviet threat, is as good as anything like it on Earth, and the claim that workmanship is shoddy, production is unreliable and working designs are inferior is totally false. As with the production of high-power microwave and millimetre-wave systems for radio high-frequency weapons, things of which the Russians were unaware only a short time ago, the ability to learn and adapt and move quickly to production is not matched in many Western countries.

But there remain areas where the Soviets require free-world expertise even though they may possess the fundamentals. Probably in due course their R&D might be able to resolve the riddles but, looking at the Soviet Union as a nation in a great hurry, it becomes understandable why it has turned its vast Intelligence community into collectors of high-tech.

It has spent a great amount of money, time and talent researching the development of particle-beam weaponry.

There has been progress but the clear leadership in this field is held by the West. Particle-beam weapons are capable of delivering intense energy particles at the speed of light – 186,000 miles a second. In theory they can penetrate solid exteriors to destroy munitions and fuels by explosion. In a peripheral sense they can destroy tremendous numbers of people. Intelligence projections for Soviet success in this area give the late 1990s as the probable date when Soviet scientists will be able to perfect such weaponry and in due course see it go into production. There is reason to believe that, as a result of recent KGB acquisitions of particle-beam technology, those Intelligence estimates may be ten years late.

In the field of comprehensive propulsion the Soviets are masters. Their R&D has contributed to the production of propellent fuels for use by land-forces and naval vessels which the West has not had to devote much time to because in the West propulsion was resolved years ago, although experimentation continues where new and better fuels are required, as in air-shuttles, long-range lunar explorers and inter-continental missiles.

In this region Soviet R&D has for some time been engaged in the development of non-traditional forms of engines, including improvement of their excellent gas-turbine power plants for naval vessels and their experimental turbo-jet aircraft engines. They have extended this variety of R&D to include feasibility work on ram-jet power plants for use in high-speed, low-level cruise missiles and long-range air-to-surface missiles. They have also advanced in the production of liquid propellent rocket engines, which are not state-of-the-art and which are designed for multiple use.

Soviet on-going R&D on sophisticated rubber-based aggregate propellents has kept pace with their successful effort to control fuel burning with inhibitors in order to extend the distance of missiles.

In fact, there are no fields of research pointing towards enhanced weaponry the Soviet Union is not interested in. Even neurochemistry and allied disciplines which would significantly increase the endurance of Soviet soldiers under combat conditions are part of the push toward the creation of a military machine capable of successfully engaging any foe or alliance of foes.

In munitions they have improved production for shaped-charge explosives, and they lead all nations in the effectiveness of fuel-air explosive power of ammunition for use against armour, against either ships at sea or tanks on land.

All Soviet R&D is conducted under restricted conditions, as they usually are in the free nations, with the most palpable difference being that penetration in the Soviet Union is next to impossible while in the West any number can play, usually do and very often win.

Until recently the US provided Soviet shoppers with the majority of their acquired technology, and although the US drain remains very great, Soviet Intelligence has achieved notable and numerous successes in Japan and Western Europe where high technology, largely under US aegis, has taken root and flourished.

They judge their technical and production standards according to a comparison with free-world achievements, perhaps unaware – or possibly indifferent about – how horse-races of this kind ordinarily end: in this instance, with someone pressed for space to store an enormous clutter of weapons that have been superseded by new, better and more sophisticated weapons which must be neutralized or matched, regardless of how long they must emulate the dog chasing his tail, until they come face to face with bankruptcy which would inhibit the pursuit and create a very real crisis, unless of course they awaken to the only alternative, providing they do not already know what it is, but in either case committed to a choice of alternatives madmen and no others would consider.

A representative example of how thorough Soviet efforts at acquisition have been has to do with their acquisition of the shaped-charge warhead for use against armour. This weapon was first developed in the West during World War II as anti-tank ammunition. It was subsequently acquired by the oil and mining industries for opening stratas of rock, for use in clearing perforated pipe casing and for clearing blast furnaces.

Between the Second World War and the recent past the shaped-charge principle was improved upon by industry as well as by US government agencies and a number of universities whose curriculum included courses where such an explosive might be needed. Over a long period the shaped-charge was modified to industrial use. Improvements were written about it and appeared in open publications. Soviet institutes engaged in underground exploration, oil and mining obtained the literature and passed it to Soviet military R&D, where it was re-modified to its original purpose and put into production to become part of the Soviet stockpile of weapons.

There are very few things which do not interest Soviet R&D institutes, even something they must have known about as far back as the Second World War and which may have subsequently been forgotten until, as an adjunct of the oil and mining industries, it re-surfaced in the civil sector. They are gleaners, overlooking very little which might have a direct or end-use military function. They have become better than the Japanese at copying. The Soviet An-72/Coaler transport aeroplane is a copy of the US Boeing Yc-14, and the Soviet 11-76/Candid is a copy of the American Lockheed C-141 'workhorse' transport aircraft. The Candid has been modified to serve as an AWAC patrol and warning aircraft, this capability made possible through Intelligence acquisitions from the West.

Their R&D is very competent, and their collection sector with years of experience is perhaps the best in the world, although to a great extent this may be the result of Western disarray in the face of the unprecedented number of Soviet shoppers.

Their production capability is impressive. Between a very good R&D, an experienced, if not always subtle Intelligence community and a superior manufacturing sector, the Soviets have managed to arm themselves with good equipment, although the quality, until recently, has not kept pace with the quantity, while simultaneously organizing the Soviet client states of the Warsaw Pact countries of Eastern Europe – Poland, Hungary, Bulgaria, Czechoslovakia, Romania and the German Democratic Republic – in the Soviet image, with the result that between the Warsaw Pact nations and the Soviet Union an unprecedented amount of weaponry has been produced and distributed worldwide.

A high percentage of conventional weapon exports to the Third World, terrorist organizations and insurrectionary movements comes from Eastern bloc countries, which is consistent with the Soviet policy of promoting instability without having to provide all the material, which leaves the Soviets breathing space to pursue R&D in areas of unconventional weaponry for use in future wars.

Nevertheless, the high degree of Soviet capability is reflected in the fact that in 1982 the USSR supplied thirty-seven per cent of all arms delivered to developing countries, which means the Soviets were able to pursue their national armaments goals while simultaneously providing other nations with more military hardware than anyone else could, or would, provide, and at the same time to expand their R&D in order that it would become even more sophisticated. There may be no better indication that Russian R&D is very good, and those who imply otherwise are mistaken.

That all this may become a victim of economics may very well be but in the past and at the present time a slackening process is scarcely discernible. In fact, while the Soviet Union's leaders have rarely demonstrated fiscal knowledgeability and at times the economy has faltered, the goal of something better than simple armed equality, while occasionally reflecting a little belt-tightening, has never been lost sight of. The R&D and S&T, as well as the Intelligence budgets, have been supplied with whatever funding they required – especially but not exclusively the Intelligence services, for without them R&D and S&T and a wide range of other things would falter. The Intelligence function seems to be what keeps all the rest of it operable. It is the 'support system' mentioned earlier. Without it R&D could hardly have achieved many of its accomplishments, and here at least the West is better informed but perhaps not as well as it might be.

What some Western leaders have seen as a Soviet espionage drive to acquire diplomatic or strategic information has become something else as well. In fact, Soviet policy appears to reflect a more contemporary view: defeating the free societies has only a peripheral concern with numbers because in military manpower the USSR has 4.4 millions, the US has 2.1 millions, and NATO forces versus the Warsaw Pact force is equally as encouraging from the Russian viewpoint.

In combat aircraft, fighting ships, and missiles the Soviets hold a scant margin in some categories, a very large margin in others. In missiles the Soviets are far ahead; in battle tanks the Warsaw Pact Alliance can field 42,600 to NATO's 13,500. In anti-tank guided weapon-launchers, Warsaw Pact 32,000, NATO 12,300. In army divisions NATO can field 86, Warsaw Pact 176. Combat vehicles: NATO 35,700, Warsaw Pact 75,000. Artillery: NATO 11,500, Warsaw Pact 35,000.

This aspect at least of the overall Soviet strategic goal has been redressed. What has obsessed Soviet leaders recently is the free-world's ability to come up with weapons which would erase their clear superiority. A decade or so ago it was announced that Soviet R&D had devised a coating for tanks which would protect them against nuclear fall-out. Ten years later, with that danger lessened and the prospect for land wars increased, it has become imperative that Soviet R&D be supplied with hard intelligence about laser weapons which might be capable of destroying a thousand battle tanks the way people water their gradens, by simply swinging the nozzle back and forth – not that any such weapon exists but the Soviets cannot be sure of that. This is the crux of the problem, and toward resolving it their Intelligence community, which once did indeed tiptoe along the back stairs of chancelleries, now subscribes to and reads tons of Western technical journals and works at recruiting people who do not wear uniforms of live in embassies.

It also pays particular attention to one of the most unique books ever published, a volume as thick as a telephone directory consisting of twenty-seven chapters entitled simply 'the Red Book'. It is highly restricted. In fact, it has only been issued to Soviet embassies and trade delegations whose acquisition of free-world technology has over the years been satisfactorily productive. It is the Kremlin's 'shopping list' of items spies are to acquire. Agents have a quota: they are annually to steal four items listed in the book, and if they succeed in acquiring high-priority items, they will '... earn prestige'. Articles listed cover sophisticated missile guidance systems as well as agricultural machinery and range from the technology for starting mititary vehicles in cold weather to tractor hydraulic systems. Much of what is listed will perhaps be acquired by the kind of seemingly apolitical, non-military agent of which a sixty-year-old German named Manfred Rotsch was typical.

Rotsch was chief of aircraft engineering for West Germany's largest arms manufacturer, Messerschmitt-Bölkow-Blohm. He was one of a very few Soviet agents abroad who was permitted to forward Western scientific and technical secrets directly to the KGB's Department T (see Chapter 10). He was in a position of access to some of the West's most closely guarded military secrets, including the specifications of the Tornado supersonic fighter aircraft, a joint development of Britain, Italy and Germany, one of NATO's most advanced jetfighters. Messerschmitt-Bölkow-Blohm also manufactured two particularly efficient anti-tank missiles, the 'HOT' and Milon projectiles, the Korman air-to-surface missile, advanced armour-piercing shells and at least two advanced military aircraft of which one was an armoured military helicopter.

Executives of Manfred Rotsch's status have access to sophisticated technology developed by the American National Aeronautics and Space Administration (NASA).

The damage someone of Rotsch's status could do to Western defence was incalculable, particularly if his espionage was of long-standing.

In Rotsch's case the Federal Republic of Germany's counter-intelligence agency uncovered evidence that he had been a Soviet agent for seventeen years, from 1967 until his apprehension in the autumn of 1984. But in fact Manfred Rotsch came to West Germany from Soviet East Germany much earlier, in 1956, and there was an excellent possibility that he was a deliberate plant whose rise to executive status within the Messerschmitt-Bölkow-Blohm organization was made possible by a Soviet mole who already possessed

executive status with the company. If so, Rotsch, the plant,
followed a classic pattern: having settled in a suburb of
Munich with his wife and three children, he became active in
the anti-Communist Christian Social Union organization. He
also joined other social associations including a chess club.
The Rotsch image was meticulously established. Neighbours
considered him a pleasant, conservative, rather colourless
individual who was civic-minded, respectable and quite ordinary. But Manfred Rotsch was neither an ambiguous amateur at his trade nor a late recruit. Nor apparently did he have
to work very hard to achieve his exalted position with West
Germany's largest arms manufacturer, as was suggested by a
subsequent investigation by West German Intelligence authorities. His procedure for acquiring secret information included photographing restricted documents, plans and
specification and passing most of them to Soviet controls he
met either in Munich or in countries where he was autho-
rized to travel on business.

After Rotsch's apprehension in late 1984, the customary
veil of secrecy descended. It included the playing-down of
damage to Western security. A Messerschmitt-Bölkow-
Blohm spokesman called the affair '. . . more important
politically than it is technically', which was asking a lot to
expect a very widespread belief that anyone who had spied
for at least seventeen years, much of it while in positions of
executive status, had not seriously compromised Western
security. Nor was it palatable that, although Rotsch was under suspicion for two years before being taken into custody,
he was not under close surveillance until two months before
he was arrested.

The case of Manfred Rotsch is not the only instance – far
from it – which would suggest that Western security leaves a
lot to be desired. If, as some Western Intelligence agencies
suspect, there are no fewer than twelve thousand active suppliers of information to the Soviets in the German Federal
Republic, even assuming that most will not have achieved
the status of Rotsch in German industry, it would appear that
the haemorrhage of free-world secrets will not end until the
Soviets, not the West, decide to end it.

10
The Support System

William Webster, director of the Federal Buerau of Investigation (FBI), said in 1981, 'I think you would be astonished by the voraciousness of ... [the Soviet] ... information gatherers.'

As a result of Press releases, by 1984 the degree of public surprise should have been minimal. Even before that time it was fairly obvious that the world's largest Intelligence network was moving into areas of espionage not traditionally associated with Intelligence operations, certainly not to the extent which subsequently became the case, and when a popular US periodical stated in 1981 the reason for this, 'In the view of strategic experts there is no other way for the Soviets to keep pace with their military and economic adversaries ...', it half stated the situation.

In an ensuing paragraph the same periodical quoting the same experts stated that, '... socialist economies, rigidly controlled from the top down are less capable of the kinds of technological innovation that are common in the West. By stealing the West's most advanced ideas, the Soviet leaders can enjoy the fruits of the capitalist system without loosening their tight political grip on society.'

The implications are that the Soviets cannot innovate or keep pace. Certainly the Soviets have been unable to innovate on an equal scale with free societies and certainly Communist countries have controlled societies. However, within the framework of what is permissible in the Soviet Union, 'pace' has been kept with the West albeit through acquired technologies and techniques, and these have opened doors Soviet scientists and engineers have moved through to demonstrate indigenous innovativeness, enough of it to put Soviet satellites aloft, Soviet navies in every sea and high-tech weaponry elsewhere, much of it considerably improved over what was acquired from the West. This has been and still appears to be, the common mistake. Soviet R&D was dependent upon free-world high technology. Presently it is so much less so that to believe otherwise is to perpetuate a fallacy.

Nor is the current purpose of Soviet Intelligence exclusively to acquire Western technology, although that is a high-priority function, the one dominating all others.

The other function is to monitor societies whose high technology progresses by leaps and bounds and will eventually without much doubt develop systems to neutralize and perhaps destroy entire armies and conceivably whole societies without leaving the ground or making a sound.

Seventy-five thousand combat vehicles or 35,000 artillery pieces would be of little use if there was no one available to operate them, and that is important to those who own the vehicles and the guns. For that reason, especially, the KGB and its consort the GRU, the Soviet Military Intelligence directorate, do not rest.

Also, as with Hitler's race with the US Manhattan Project to build the world's first atomic bomb, Soviet leaders do not want to be, as Hitler was, second-guessers. Therefore while they digest enormous amount of Western technology, much of it adaptable to their military needs, Russian R&D awaits the arrival of the ultimate ground weapon. It would be a mistake to believe R&D scientists in the Soviet Union are not capable of taking someone else's theoretical physics to its ultimate goal or of perfecting their own.

The spectre to haunt Soviet leaders is the knowledge that it would be impossible to wage a war or to win one if an adversary had the ability to destroy the best that their army had. More to the point, it would be inconceivable to engage such an adversary unless it was known such weaponry existed and to obtain or duplicate it for first use.

Anyone, including Soviet war-hawks and in spite of ruthless intransigence, understands the meaning of defeat.

As long as this fear exists to haunt those with the largest armies and arsenals, spies will neglect the chancelleries in favour of the laboratories – most certainly to steal high technology but particularly to watch for the weapon which could turn a twenty-year accumulation of expensive heavy hardware into a junk pile.

Meanwhile the quest for less exotic high-tech continues, often with a lack of finesse which earns Western scorn, although while clumsy spies are caught with routine regularity, obviously a greater majority have been neither clumsy nor caught, otherwise that overwhelming array of advanced Soviet military power would not exist, although a number of authorities claim that most of what the USSR has acquired in the West has been obtained legally, which may be open to debate since acquisitions have increased since formation of the free-world's embargo systems.

But that does not affect the clandestine operations run by the KGB and GRU. Nor does the routine uncovering of their agents deter them. Intelligence agencies which employ thousands are unlikely to be upset by the exposure of a few. In 1983 the US quietly expelled five Soviet citizens. From nineteen countries a total of 135 Soviet diplomatic and commercial personnel left voluntarily or were expelled that same year. This number may reflect an increase in the number of spies. It may also reflect a decline in the quality of Soviet secret agents. But whatever it signifies, only twenty-seven were expelled in 1980 and only forty-nine in 1982, so the 135 expulsions in 1983 suggest that Soviet Intelligence had a busy year. It may also indicate that expulsions and probably tighter export controls have not bothered KGB or GRU authorities in Moscow, where the organizations – the 'support systems' – which compile shopping lists and send forth the locusts are permanently headquartered. Nor are these Soviet establishments, like the German school at Bad Oldesloe, new in the neighbourhood.

The KGB is huge. Since 1922, when the Soviet national security apparatus was called the NKVD or People's Commissariat of Internal Affairs, the power and size of Soviet Intelligence have grown considerably. Each time there was organizational re-structuring it grew still more. In 1923 the NKVD was divided but in 1934 under Josef Stalin it was reorganized to include former divisions and new responsibilities. It controlled the Police, border guards, labour camps and internal troops, even a number of business enterprises and some areas of the national transportation system.

By 1941 the NKVD had supervision of concentration camps and was the watchdog of Soviet industry. In 1946, after more reorganizing, the NKVD, along with other, off-shoot organizations, became a state ministry. One section, the KGB, had a number of foreign departments.

Eventually the NKVD became the MVD or Ministry of Internal Affairs but more re-structuring, the result of the Cold War among other things, resulted in the establishment of a new organization, the KI or Committee of Information. KI, which was directly responsible to Stalin, assumed some of the responsibilities of the Soviet Foreign Ministry – the equivalent of Britain's MI5 supervising the Foreign Office or the CIA supervising the US State Department. It also took over the GRU, the military's Intelligence service. And it more than doubled in size. In 1948 KI lost GRU responsibility back to the army. In 1951 Stalin abolished KI, and the MGB surfaced as the bureau in charge of overseas clandestine operations.

When Stalin died in 1953, a consolidation of Intelligence reorganizations began which ended with the GRU confirmed as the Military Intelligence agency and the KGB with traditional police functions, which, in the Soviet Union, included responsibility for all clandestine operations abroad except those run by Military Intelligence – the GRU.

In 1973 the KGB became a State Ministry under Yuri Andropov. It had unlimited internal and external power with a complement of approximately 700,000, 300,000 of which were Soviet Border Guards, the KGB's private army, which also included a small force of naval ships. The Border Guards as an elite corps were provided with the best available weapons as well as advanced electronic surveillance and detection equipment.*

When foreign Intelligence agencies go up against the Soviet KGB, they face the largest Intelligence organization

---

* The best available books about the KGB are Walter Conquest's *The Great Terror* and John Barron's *KGB*.

that ever existed. The CIA, largest of Western Intelligence agencies, is about one-tenth the size of the KGB and, granting that size does not guarantee efficiency – in this case quite the contrary, it does guarantee that the plague of locusts can overwhelm smaller, more efficient Intelligence organizations which cannot be everywhere at the same time. To a degree, that is exactly what has made the drain of high technology from free societies like a haemorrhage.

Under the KGB's First Chief Directorate it was Directorate T, the Scientific and Technical Directorate, that was responsible for the theft of Western data about the strategic sciences, nuclear, missile and space research. Directorate T inaugurated and supervised clandestine acquisition operations and co-ordinated the scientific, technical and industrial espionage of all other KGB bureaus. It was staffed by knowledgeable personnel in most of these specialities, and because of this it has been a long time since blackmarket brokers in foreign countries could sell random acquisitions to the Soviet Union.

Directorate T, which has four separate departments, was one of thirteen departments of the First Chief Directorate, each with its own individual departments.* It worked closely with the State Scientific and Technical Committee (GNTK) which had charge of allocating scientific resources.

GNTK, in conjunction with Directorate T and other KGB departments, decided when to send Soviet scientific delegations outside the country, to trade fairs and scientific conferences, and also to evaluate foreign high-tech systems. When these parties went abroad, they were accompanied by KGB personnel from either Directorate T, GNTK or other KGB bureaus.

GNTK, like Directorate T, had access to the most knowledgeable scientists in the USSR, and although like other organizations which serve KGB interests it was not a part of the KGB, it might as well have been.

Since being established in 1972, about the time a flood of free-world technology began to inundate KGB departments

* The first Chief Directorate is thought by some to consist of sixteen departments.

which had not been established specifically to handle high technology, Directorate T grew until it had, aside from a staff of hundreds, specialists masquerading as diplomats, embassy staffers and commercial attachés in all the important Soviet foreign embassies. These have been the agents who evaluated what clandestine brokers had to offer and who handed out the shopping lists covering items required by the USSR's scientific and military communities. In addition Directorate T has used the services of both the R&D and S&T sectors in advisory positions and to reinforce its own opinions and judgements.

Its effectiveness could be measured by the successful integration of illegally obtained nuclear, space, cybernetic and industrial technologies into the Soviet military complex.

It also has a close connection with other departments of the First Chief Directorate, but its importance as an individual bureau was exemplified by the fact that Special Services I, the KGB information bureau, which gathered and distributed information obtained by the First Chief Directorate, did not have jurisdiction over Directorate T's information processes.

There is a lack of general confirmation that Directorate T used the ten KGB geographic departments which are also part of the First Chief Directorate, but a very strong possibility exists that it did.

The first of the geographic bureaus covered the US and Canada. The third bureau covered Great Britain, Scandinavia, New Zealand and Australia. The seventh bureau covered much of Asia including Japan, while the fourth and fifth bureaus covered Western Europe – the Federal Republic of Germany, Luxembourg, France, Austria, Italy, Spain, the Netherlands, Belgium and Ireland. Within these areas are where the world's most advanced technologies exist, and the geographic departments were staffed by personnel knowledgeable about them. Many have served as diplomats, attachés or commercial agents, or in other capacities outside the Soviet Union.

After the end of the Second World War the main targets of Soviet espionage were the US, the British Commonwealth, West Germany and Japan. After 1960 the areas of vital concern included countries such as Canada, Mexico, Iran, Iraq, Greece and Turkey, but for political reasons. By the late 1960s interest in Latin America increased, but again for political reasons, and this was not the concern of Directorate T. But simultaneously with the interest in Latin America, as the high technology of the territories originally targeted the US, Japan, the British Commonwealth and West Germany advanced to unprecedented levels of sophistication they once again became priority targets this time less for political or military reasons than for their technology. The secret agents who had formerly sought military secrets were now outnumbered by those seeking something quite different, and while some nations – the US for example – were satisfied to employ analysts to perform as wizards, and by deducing from collections of information what was occurring behind the Iron Curtain, the Russians chose to follow a different course.

Although they followed the US example of using sky-spies, electronic eavesdropping equipment and con-versation-monitors, they really depended upon the human agent. Their reasoning seemed to be that analysis was likely to be unreliable if not downright wrong. General Alexander Orlov, who defected to the West more than a generation ago and who wrote a Soviet espionage manual, set forth the Soviet opinion of second-guess Intelligence: 'When the Russians want to know the number of bombers in the air force of a potential adversary, they arrive at a figure – not by library research on the production capacity of certain plants or by collecting educated guesses or rumours on the subject but by interviewing their secret informers in the foreign office or war ministry and by stealing the coveted information from government files.' This, the General said, was regarded by the Soviets as 'real' Intelligence. (Others use the term 'hard' Intelligence.) They regarded all other kinds as 'research data' and not only distrusted it but thought little of those who based judgements upon it.*

This policy has certainly put forth a great many agents. The collection of 'hard' Intelligence requires nothing less,

---

* The CIA relies heavily on this kind of 'analytical' data.

and the débâcles are proportionate to the numbers. Also, because it requires informers, it ensures that target nations catch a lot of their own citizens working for Soviet Intelligence. In 1980 Finland sentenced a citizen to prison for passing secrets to his Russian control, and near the end of February of the same year the French expelled a Soviet Press attaché, Viatcheslav Frolov, who was apprehended in possession of the plans and specifications of the ultra-secret French Mirage 2000 jet fighter aircraft which he had acquired through native sources.

In January 1980 the Canadians expelled three Russians, Colonel Eduard Aleksanian, Captain Igor Bardeev and an embassy chauffeur, R. I. Sokolov, for attempting to purchase US secrets through a US citizen of official status.

Concurrent with the expulsion of seven Soviet spies from Spain in 1980 (three years after those countries had re-established diplomatic relations) the Dutch tightened their security because a Soviet trade delegation had tried earlier to obtain information about their advanced chemical industry from native sources.

Arkady Shevchenko, a Soviet United Nations diplomat who defected to the United States in 1978, told a US House of Representatives sub-committee that about half of the Russians assigned to the UN mission in New York were engaged in espionage. Intelligence sources estimate that an even higher percentage – sixty-five per cent – were in the same category at the Washington embassy.

It was Americans who passed information about the A-bomb to Soviet agents. When President Roosevelt described the awesome power of this new Western weapon to Marshal Stalin in the 1945 Yalta Conference, Stalin was not awed. He already knew about America's A-bomb.

The Soviet policy on 'hard' Intelligence cannot be faulted. Despite the routine discovery of its aims and its agents, its success as a policy is not arguable. This has been recognized by adversary Intelligence services who have been unable either to match the numbers of Soviet agents or to penetrate the closed society of Russia with anything like the ease with which the Soviets have penetrated the free societies with their greater numbers.

Soviet espionage has assumed such proportions that it is routinely attributed with a great deal it was not involved in. Newspapers print very unlikely stories based upon someone's paranoid idea of what might have occurred. On 6 March 1980 the London *Daily Express* ran a story suggesting that the Soviets had arranged the marriage of a Russian, Sergei Kauzov, and Greek shipping heiress Christina Onassis in 1978 so that Russian authorities could obtain information concerning Western oil resources. Kauzov, according to the article, was a suspected KGB agent.

Occasionally inaccuracies or improbabilities work in favour of Soviet Intelligence, although having the reputation of being the nation least to be trusted makes it more probable that even natural disasters can be attributed to the Russians without arousing much disagreement. If this causes dismay in the USSR, its political and Intelligence authorities have concealed it well.

They do not withdraw support from agents running acquisition operations, and, because the penalty if caught ordinarily amounts to nothing more than expulsion, as opposed to official and public uproar in former times if a project fails, exposed agents are flown home to be reassigned, and if the project is important a new approach using different agents begins. But regardless of failures it is inherent in the system to persevere. This identical pertinacity characterizes the entire Soviet system and has since its inception, when Lenin stated that it would be impossible for Capitalism and Communism to co-exist. One must destroy the other. On that basis, plus one other, the Russians do not give up. The other basis for Soviet perseverance is the acceptance of long-term objectives. In their certainty of triumph the same words have been used for more than a half century: eventually, ultimately, terminally.

With that variety of endemic philosophy it should surprise no one that they have never abandoned either a political or Intelligence objective, neither those which have required decades to achieve nor those which have failed.

On the Intelligence front this doggedness has made one thing obvious: as long as the Soviet Intelligence support system continues to come to the West for acquisition of the world's best technology, it obviously has failed to achieve parity in this area at home, and as long as it relies on the free-world and feels compelled to do so, the Intelligence war possibly will not become a shooting war. As long as free-world sophisticated technology continues to produce one marvel after another, each better – or worse – than those which have preceded it, Soviet shoppers will continue to arrive. It is a foot-race without a discernible end, a silent and frantic pursuit during which the pursuer fears desperately he will be unable to overtake the pursued.

For twenty years the Soviets have exulted; their enormous support system has achieved one *coup* after another, computers, lasers, electronic marvels, land, sea and air techniques undreamed of fifty years ago – but they are still running. The free societies do not infiltrate the Soviet Union even though Russian research and development have made tremendous strides; instead they put regiments of their own Intelligence agents into the free societies. For a generation and more they have been the jackals, the highly trained, well-funded, overpoweringly armed beggars.

The Soviet blend of political militarism which encourages this policy of pursuit is not Communism. If it were, there would have been ideological dissenters to prevent the KGB from establishing itself as a state within the state, its recently deceased leader above Soviet law, and his organization outside Party control. Nothing like this had occurred in the Soviet Union since Stalin. As long as committees ruled, with their inevitably different points of view and garrulous polemics, vintage Communist jargon filled newspapers and, despite the mighty military build-up, war was not upon the horizon; menace was, but it always had been.

During Leonid Brezhnev's tenure as Soviet leader, the shadow of Yuri Andropov lengthened. During Brezhnev's decline the centre of power in the Soviet Union perceptibly shifted from the Central Committee to the KGB. Brezhnev's 'nyet' was superseded by the silence of the man who ruled behind Brezhnev's back, Andropov.

Détente died, dissent was crushed, expansionism (Afghanistan), repression (of Jews) and the Intelligence sectors growth signalled an era of evident change. Andropov, with his huge police-state organization, had no trouble with the Central Committee. He ruled Russia.

His deputy, General Semyon Tsvigun, tried to intervene when Andropov ordered the arrest of friends of Brezhnev's daughter. He was found in the office with a bullet in his head. To secure the KGB's overriding authority, Andropov as Premier appointed KGB officers to strategic posts. Vitaly Fedorchuk, one-time chief of the Ukrainian secret police, became Minister of Internal Affairs. Victor Chebrykov, Andropov's KGB deputy, became head of the KGB. Geidar Aliyev, former head of the Azerbaijan KGB, became deputy chairman of the USSR Council of Ministers, a full member of the Politburo.

What Andropov accomplished before his death was the nucleus of a total KGB state without an ideology, simply a police state. Since his passing efforts at dismantling the apparatus have not surfaced.

Men such as Marshal Ustinov and Yuri Andropov did not need the façade or its basis, and because of this others may very well find that the Russian attitude will be more harsh inside the country and more aggressive elsewhere. They will also find, as many already have, that the Intelligence function will increase and become more aggressive in its methods.

There is a corollary here. The anxiety born of fear may end, which has kept the Soviet support system running to the West in order not to have some ultimate weapons system become productive there, without Soviet knowledge. Dmitry Ustinov was not a temporizing warrior. Neither are Naval Forces Commander-in-Chief S.G. Gorshkov and A.A. Yepishev, Chief, Main Political Directorate. There is reason to believe that these men or their successors might not be influenced by the existence of a new and exotic weapon or by disarmament talks but rather by a conviction that they are powerful enough to prevail even if their adversaries had such a weapon. These are the men who consider nuclear bombs nothing more than an extenuation of artillery, which must be the philosophy of trash-burners.

Nevertheless, the Intelligence pursuit continues greater than before, and as a system of support for procurement of high technology through various sources it is very successful.

There are no better agents in the world than those of the Soviet Union; their techniques have been perfected through fifty years of trial and error. As with Soviet research and development, ridiculed for so long as being backward, the Russian Intelligence sector is as good as any Intelligence organization and vastly superior to most of those owned by nations whose job has been to halt the technology haemorrhage and who have demonstrated their inferiority by being unable to do so.

11
Hyperboreans and Others

If the elements of free societies which have opposed embargoes of high technology and restrictions upon the free exchange of ideas have done so from practical as opposed to altruistic motives, realization must be imminent that in a politicized world there is no such thing as international goodwill; at best there is only international accord.

In both the scientific and academic communities where denunciation of controls has been particularly strident, non-empiricists have extolled open exchange, insisted upon freedom from control, denounced censorship and sought recognition of New Age apostles of worldwide free thought with the privilege of unrestricted exchange.

Two Americans of note have been especially outspoken in this regard, Albert Einstein and Victor Weisskopf. Like others who have insisted that scientific discovery belongs to all the world to be shared openly, Einstein and Weisskopf achieved arcane formulas for arriving at their distinctions about this. Scientific knowledge belongs to all the world – but not of course to Hitler's Germany, which was bad; yet it should be shared with Soviet Russia. The tidy conclusion ended as a conundrum: was there really a difference between what is bad and what is not good?

For Albert Einstein disillusionment may have come late; for others it appears not to have arrived at all. Einstein, the pure scientist, could say, 'The Lord may be subtle but He is not malicious,' and see nothing irreconcilable between his belief and his vocation which routinely doubted belief. For others including Victor Weisskopf altruism appeared to derive from different motives and be subject to a different interpretation. Weisskopf evidently believed in practical applications. As Chairman of the US High Energy Physics

Advisory Panel of the Atomic Energy Commission, he made it possible for the Soviet Union to build its Serpukhov lineal accelerator, giving the enemies of free exchange a quantum jump in their search for sophisticated methods of weapons enhancement.

Since then it has become increasingly difficult for some scientists and academics to uphold pure altruism while looking down the gun-barrels of fifty thousand Soviet tanks, but some persevere, labouring somewhere between Einstein and Weisskopf, believing pure science has no nationality, that they are special people belonging to a different class and in this perhaps finding comfort in the Marxist dictum which states that the bond between the same class in different countries is likely to be stronger than the bond between different classes in the same country.

Such intrusions into the lives of academics and scientists as security investigations have aroused both ire and denunciation. For years there was little in the way of restrictions or intrusions because there was no general concern they might be desirable. From those times arose the idea of altruistic exchange, and although those times are no longer with us, their innocence seems to be.

Pure scientists who lived for their work had need of an environment free of ordinary anxieties. Coming out of intense preoccupation over such obscure matters as the fate of Schrödinger's cat to face the real world presented them with a very unwelcome confrontation – they did not live in Hyperborea after all, that land beyond the North Wind of eternal sunlight and magnificent serenity where everyone was altruistic. And their indignation, as well as their defections, has more often than not had nothing to do with disbelief in political systems; it arose from the intense disappointment which followed the discovery that they did not live in Hyperborea.

A native of the Ukraine who was also a US citizen, Orest Makar, lived and worked in the US after 1949. He had security clearance, achieved prominence in the missile field, was knowledgeable about US IBM Titans and Atlases and was also an authority on photography. He had been employed at Alamagordo, where the first atomic bomb was developed.

Makar's list of achievements was impressive. He worked for eight months at the White Sands, New Mexico, missile-testing facility and was a physicist for the US Air Force as well as a mathematical consultant. He was a pure scientist. Like others in his category Makar was paid well while in government service. He had none of the worries ordinary people had who were not guaranteed the security which went with high-paying government employment until he ventured into the private sector.

There in the real world Orest Makar's confrontation with reality left him appalled. In that environment people put on tin beaks and got down to scratch with the chickens. They had to produce, to obey the laws of supply and demand. Their work was subject to critical review. Unlike the world of science, life at the competitive levels was not a law unto itself. In a competitive society people were responsible for themselves, and hypothetical ratiocination, as beautiful, almost lyrical, as it was, was no guarantee of employment.

Professor Makar was neither a Communist nor a Capitalist. He was a scientist. Science was his life – under ideal working conditions. In 1956 he was invited to attend an international conference in Sweden. He left the US with his wife Alexandra and gave several lectures on photography in Stockholm, and he did not return. He met Soviet scientists in Stockholm. This was the kind of meeting they attended. 'While following scientific literature in my own field,' he said later, 'I found that science is being taken very seriously there [in the USSR] and that the best working conditions for scientific research work exist in the Soviet Union.'

He asked for asylum at the Soviet Embassy. He said, 'They more than met me half way,' which seemed reasonable since Professor Makar was an authority on US missilry, defence, research and production. At debriefings he could provide worthwhile information. But to Orest Makar, whose need was to work at his specialities in an atmosphere free of everyday anxieties, what he undoubtedly told Soviet interrogators created no crisis of conscience; he was a scientist, and pure science belonged to all mankind.

In the USSR the designation 'scientist' confers rank and

privileges rarely matched in the West. Soviet scientists are given cars with drivers, comfortable apartments, adequate salaries, tax privileges, social acceptance, preferred treatment; occasionally they are also given country homes. They do not have to wait in line; they are relieved of the worries of everyday living and receive full support for their work. Competitiveness, academic demands and niggling supervision do not exist. Security and advancement even for pure theorists are assured.

Of course belief in free exchange does not exist either, and there is the requirement of absolute secrecy. Nor are enquiries into matters outside one's own speciality, nor having coffee with foreigners, encouraged. On the other hand scientists are absolved from obligation to Party dogma ordinary Soviet citizens share. They are not required to be dogmatists; they simply have to do their work. All Soviet science is oriented toward Soviet advancement.

Orest Makar became, as many pure scientists have dreamed of becoming, outside the political world, beyond the *mores* of a structured society. In the Soviet Union, because of the nature of their profession and the State's need to know, scientists have degrees of support and respect most believe they are entitled to, and for defecting scientists such as Orest Makar who are apolitical and whose life is their work there is no need to sublimate the conscience because it was never in trouble.

If working conditions in the USSR are so ideal, why do not more Western scientists defect? They do. For years it has been Soviet policy to make certain scientists in the West know of the excellent working conditions for scientists in the USSR. Probably more Western scientists have defected than people in any other category, and this has had a significant impact on Soviet progress in all scientific fields. It most certainly has been largely responsible for the great strides science and technology have made over the last decade; and the knowledge they have brought with them has presented the Soviets with an excellent understanding of Western advances.

Soviet scientists who visit foreign conferences have provided forums for a comparison of the scientific systems.

They have also provided the routines to be employed for defection. They represent one segment of an international fraternity: an association of enquirers whose discipline can transcend nationality and which in the Soviet Union is ordinarily concerned with neither the price of bread nor political systems.

In comparison free societies do not fare very well. The budget director in the West who refuses to allocate funds for theoretical research if it cannot promise to provide early and practical results has no Soviet counterpart. Nor are there the same demands as in the USSR for academic scientists to publish books or in other ways to bring renown and its accompanying financial contributions to their institutions.

Further, scientific research in the Soviet Union, where power and prestige are an obsession, will be funded for varieties of research the West rarely even acknowledges. A Soviet scientist worked for years to develop an engine that would use time for fuel. Russian scientists have government-supported facilities for enquiries into such fields as telepathy, mind-reading, even palmistry and séances, fields of research not generally viewed favourably elsewhere – certainly not by industry and only slightly more favourably by governments, although there have been exceptions.

Not long ago a Hungarian physicist fled his country for the US. His professional qualifications were excellent but he had an aberration Hungarian Communists disapproved of. He was into communicating with the dead, something considered unbecoming in a scientist. In the US he was offered employment by a large company of the private sector to whom his professional qualifications were valuable. If he chose to hold séances and in other ways to contact dead people on his own time, the company had no objection. In fact, it offered to provide some of the equipment he needed. This was an exception to the general rule, and perhaps if it demonstrated anything it may have been that there was less of a broadening of viewpoints than a willingness to overlook peculiarities for the sake of obtaining valuable services. For the Hungarian it meant that scientists, whether heading East or West, are far less concerned with whose flag is overhead than that they will be free to pursue their enquiries. But the lure of vocation-related perquisites has enticed a great many scientists away from the West and certainly will continue to do so. Others, such as academics whose altruism has a less fundamental reason for objecting to restrictions, are less likely to share in the Soviet bounties of defection. Nor does it seem reasonable that they should, since their opposition is largely ideological, and if there is one commodity the Soviets have never had a shortage of or which they have never needed outsiders to help them with it has been ideology. Nor are they presently in need of it – less so now than ever. However, defectors are not welcomed whose sole contribution is an affinity with Communist dogma, although they do encourage and even to some extent fund foreign sympathizers who remain in the West and create disruptions there because they cause trouble for enemies of the Soviet Union, which is beginning to see enemies everywhere, especially among its allies by treaty.

Nevertheless, academic defiance in the free societies and particularly in areas of research, hypothesis and ideas rests upon solid ground: freedom of expression, even though those whose protests have been loudest against controls on sensitive technology have placed their inalienable rights as they interpret them above the interests and the survival of free societies. What they see as being at stake is that right of expression all free societies recognize as being one of the cornerstones of enlightened civilizations. That this freedom has been guaranteed only by the sacrifices of many or that it carries with it inherent responsibilities does not appear to impinge upon their conviction that only freedom of expression matters.

This viewpoint may arise naturally among people whose insularity has convinced them that parliamentary guarantees as well as cloistered environments are safe providing they resist even limited restrictions, or it may arise from other notions, but whatever its basis it exists in academic communities as a variety of contentiousness which adds another dimension to the problems free societies face in their effort to prevent sensitive information from reaching the enemies of free societies.

Right or wrong, it does appear that this attitude cannot be entirely curtailed without injuring the system which guarantees it. As with ideas, no effective system has been developed throughout human history to control thought or expression while at the same time serving the best interests of societal liberty. There has never been a revolutionary idea which has not left its native land nor has there ever before existed such an urgency to prevent this happening as now.

The development of unprecedented horrors has proliferated because the best security systems have failed. The idea behind the Trojan horse, the Gatling gun, the catapult, the atomic bomb – how to massacre human beings effectively – has come down the millennia intact. The catapult became a cannon, the Trojan horse became an armoured tank, the Gatling gun became the machine-gun, the atomic bomb became an arsenal of nuclear devices which at ground-level can vaporize all life – and these are only for openers.

The idea behind contemporary innovations may relegate the battle tank to the status of its ancestor the Trojan horse. Is it any more possible to keep the lid on Pandora's box now than it was then? And how can the free societies protect themselves against hordes of Soviet agents dedicated to ransacking them ruthlessly while at the same time retaining the freedoms upon which their civilization has rested for centuries? Up until now no system has prevented this ransacking even though it is common knowledge that what the Soviets have acquired has been adapted to their arsenal of menace. What will they acquire in the future because free exchange and clandestine successes have made it available to them?

In times of conflict, nations of people willingly submit to the necessity of restrictions and control because they recognize what is essential to their survival. But in conflict people also see their ships sunk, their cities bombed, their people massacred. They have yet to understand that there is such a thing as a war called peace. This being the case, they neglect collectively or voluntarily to enjoin the same rules, and meanwhile what will the enemies of free societies acquire because free exchange, clandestine successes, avarice, duplicity and tunnel vision will make it available to them?

It is obvious what they will do with what they acquire because there already is a mountain of armed hardware as evidence. What then will they acquire to add to their mountain?

Robotics for one thing. Particle-beam and advanced-laser technology for another. The general consensus has laser technology well out in front as a source for future weapons, but for this consensus to be relevant it must be determined what frame of time is meant by the term 'future?' Laser technology cannot produce any practical space or battlefield weapons in the short-term 'future'. It may never be able to, and if it does it will not do it in any form now recognizable as 'weapons'.

Possibly as a result of popular science fiction and the *Star Wars* type of motion picture where such things as 'killer laser' are made to seem realistic through sophisticated special effects, there appears to be a widespread belief in the imminence of beam weaponry. But in fact toymakers have produced something closer to what can become a practical future weapon, and in this instance 'future' means between the present time and the near future – five years. It is the robot. Free-world scientists and engineers have taken robotics out of the toymaker's shop and perfected them for industrial use. In Japan, for example, which uses three times as many robots as anyone else, it has been estimated that within a decade industrial robots will make ninety-four per cent of the labour force redundant.

12

Toward 2000

One of the most advanced facilities which manufactures robots is Japan's Dainichi Machinery Company, and there as elsewhere private sector R&D is heavily engaged in creating products which will revolutionize industry. At Dainichi industrial robots are built for general industrial trade and export.

Robots have different categories. For example, only about thirty per cent are real robots, those which can perform operations other than simple repetitive programmed movements. The remaining seventy per cent are automated single-purpose machines. They can turn a screw or tighten a bolt but they cannot align the screw or emplace the bolt. Also, most industrial robots are large, heavy machines which handle heavy steel or large frames and therefore require a strong stationary base. They cannot move or even be moved without considerable effort. They are engineered to perform one operation in the same position. They are no more than industrial machines advanced over manual drop-hammers, for instance, only because they are electronically programmed. Dainichi is working on a means to make robots ambulatory so that they will be able to move freely from one position to another. In conjunction with this there is a programme to enable robots to do more than one job – in effect to create robots to replace humans in industry.

In other countries this research is also in progress. The Soviet Union, which has legally acquired robots along with specifications and technical information, is pushing the development of military robotics.

A robot has a motor and sensory decision-making capabilities. Presently the industrial robots used in factories which tighten the bolt or turn the screw perform functions a

Toward 2000 117

human being with an Intelligence Quotient (IQ) of 70 can also do. The main difference is that if the bolt or screw falls to the floor the robot goes through its sequence regardless, where the human worker can retrieve and re-align the bolt or screw. In effect the robot is 'blind' and lacks simple instinctive reasoned responses. However, if the robot's programming is brought to an IQ level of about 90, it knows there is no bolt in the hole and will select another one from its supply of bolts, emplace it and tighten it.

The Japanese estimate is that most workers have IQs ranging between 90 and 120. The plan is to produce a robot with an IQ of about 110. With an IQ of 110, robots could perform relatively sophisticated operations, and if they could be made ambulatory as well, they could move about a factory to perfom more than one operation. What makes this possible is something which already exists, electronic memories which store past experiences for instant recall.

Special robots now in process of being developed will possess the ability to create new items but the main problem for industrial robots remains their large, heavy and stationary status and their ability to perform one simple task. In Japan, where space is limited, stationary robots that tighten one bolt at a time, even when assembly systems as well as the robots are speeded up, still only tighten the bolt. In a factory where forty or fifty manufacturing sequences are followed, forty or fifty large, heavy robots take up a great amount of space. The answer to weight and mass in the aircraft industry was lighter and stronger metals. These are being studied for their feasibility in robotic laboratories. In the US considerable progress has been made in this area.

But while weight and mass are a detriment in industrial robots, the contrary is true for military robots, where size and strength are desirable. Currently in production for industrial use are robots that weld, paint, align, crush, shape and perform a number of other operations, and each of these functions has a military end-use.

The pervading anxiety that robots will replace human beings in industry and thereby create seemingly unresolveable difficulties does not concern the military.

In industry there will be a necessary cadre of tecnhicians

to maintain the robots. In terms of military use, this translates to the same kind of advanced technology specialists programming and maintaining military robots, quite conceivably with the same problem of redundancy – millions of superfluous human beings – and while the novelty of this concept would undoubtedly appeal to millions of potential conscripts, it would probably possess little appeal for anyone else.

Projections concerning the day when practically self-contained robots exist has caused concern among the prescient and scepticism among others. As a matter of fact, that day has arrived. Many robots require a minimum of human interference. The smarter the robot, the less it requires human association. At present there are robots which can 'think' their way into large, populated cities, following roads to areas of particularly dense habitation, and when they get there use the military equivalent of the industrial paint-spraying technique to spray clouds of lethal chemicals.

In Japan a manufacturer of robots has suggested that there '... is a fundamental difference between men and machines. Robots do not have the same psychological or emotional attributes. They are not capable of producing the subtle nuances of human thought and feeling.' For those reasons, then, despite the wrenching social changes robotics will bring, they will not pose insoluble problems. The obvious fault with this logic is that what the manufacturer said about robots also applies to generals.

An American author promulgated a law for robotics: robots must not injure humans. In the US a company called Robot Defence Systems, located in Colorado, exhibited a robot in mid-June 1984 which it named 'Prowler', an acronym for Robot Observer With Logical Entry Response. Prowler resembled a small, stylized tank. The prototype had wheels with lug-type tyres but they were arranged so that with a minimum of modification they could be replaced by crawler-treads of steel, like tanks. Production Prowlers will come with distance sensors and microcomputers as well as programmable artificial intelligence software. They will patrol and identify intruders. They will be delivered with optional weaponry as requested by purchasers and can be programmed to shoot trespassers with or without human permission.

Prowler has stopping power, a grenade-launcher and two M60 machine-guns, but company spokesmen profess to see no need for such armament, at least not in the US. Elsewhere, perhaps – '... in countries where there aren't the same political or moral considerations'.

Prowlers, so their creators say, are ideal for protecting '... pipelines, air bases, palaces, where you're outnumbered'. At a cost of $200,000 each, Prowlers will probably not appear soon in residential neighbourhoods. But is it inconceivable that they were not developed for prosaic use? At $200,000 per unit, properly armed and capable of killing hundreds of people within moments, they would be a genuine bargain for KGB, Pentagon and other like-minded shoppers.

In Woburn, Massachusetts, another company, Denning Mobile Robotics, has developed a robot prison guard to patrol corridors, give voice commands and send alarms to human guards. Denning Robotics does not envision arming its robots, which were expressly designed for patrol of industrial and commercial facilities. But Denning's devices can be readily enhanced, and it would seem unlikely that any robot manufacturer would be content to sell a few units to guard pipelines or to patrol prisons, when the real money is up the road at the Pentagon or overseas in Moscow.

The field of robotics grew dramatically in the US when the Department of the Army (DOD) included in its fiscal 1985 budget a request to develop its own robot, '... an autonomous land vehicle ... capable of manoevring around an open battlefield using its own computerized intelligence'.

In May 1984 the Pentagon's Defence Advanced Research Projects Agency (DARPA) invited proposals from three large US defence firms for production of robots as part of a heavily funded, crash Strategic Computing Programme whose stated objective is to be able to '... tell a machine to go kill enemy tanks, hide, identify friend from foe, kill the enemy and scamper off'.

Presently, among commercial and industrial researchers and developers in the West, one problem has been to teach a robot how to recognize a door and open it. In the military sector this is not seen as an obstacle. Military robots will have neither to recognize the door nor to open it: they will only have to 'know' enough to blow the whole wall away.

A research scientist at an eastern US university, Hans Moravec, suggested that perhaps the best way to achieve a general artificial intelligence would be to perfect robotics. But he could not imagine arming a robot. 'I don't think anyone would allow an armed thing as stupid as a robot to be around humans.' According to the sales record of that Colorado firm, Robot Defence Systems, as well as Defence Department interest and at least one KGB attempt thus far to acquire an advanced US robot system, with specifications, the Moravec view may not be widespread.

Within three years nearly indestructible robots will be operational and deployed. According to a DOD authority, within ten years at far less than the cost of tanks thousands of military robots will be available to disable tanks, demolish grounded aircraft and in attacking waves surround cities, take entire populations hostage, destroy those who attempt to flee and in regiments invade cities using poison or mind-destroying gases to depopulate them.

It seems reasonable to suppose that into the 1990s the industrial theft and espionage which fed the underground pipeline through the previous quarter century primarily with high-tech computer information will develop an equal interest in robotics.

Robots have electronic 'brains' as do computers but robots do not require an electrical wall-plug. They have shed that particular dependency; they are free to move. If they do not quite yet possess the computer's versatile software, they soon will, although as weapons they will not require exceptional sophistication. Neither does anything else whose sole reason for existing is limited exclusively to killing.

But robotics, while certainly destined to profit from advanced computer technology and to parallel it in growth and improvement, may be a while acquiring the variety of computer high-tech presently on-going in the West and Japan, assuming that it will need it.

The heart of a computer is its memory. Until recently

research and development in this area concentrated on creating smaller and faster circuits. The most powerful memory has been the 64K dynamic RAM (Randon Access Memory) chip. Computers of all sizes depend on collections of these chips which are very small and which are first etched with integrated circuitry, then cut from large silicon wafers. This process requires painstaking detail.

For years the US dominated this field, then the Japanese captured control. When it became difficult to steal US silicon technology, Russian attention turned eastward where prospects for acquisition were better; then it was required to look both ways as a result underway in the US to develop a super memory chip. One example was the 256K, a vast improvement over the 64K. It would be more efficient, less susceptible to trouble and faster but despite these advances the 256K retained the necessity for signals to travel from one chip to another.

A main-frame computer may use as many as four thousand chips and operate at roughly fifteen MIPS (million instructions per second). With the 256K RAM chips the speed would remain the same in conventional computers but the memory – or 'mind' – would be enormously increased: computer IQs would soar. Unlike more complicated systems which have very complex circuitry, the 256K RAM chips where the 'memory' is stored were aligned in a simple array. 256K RAM chips could store 262,144 bits of information on pieces of silicon* one quarter of an inch square. Each bit of information as an integrated 'reasoning' segment of the computer's intelligence enhances its capacity for 'thought'. At 15 MIPS 256Ks could provide an intelligence superior to the human mind in response time but only in areas for which the computer has been programmed.

In military terms this means a weapons system could become more sophisticated and less dependent upon the human factor, and this is only the beginning. The search for better 'memories' has been continuous and mind-boggling. Every three or four years the amount of

---

* Silicon is actually high-grade sand that a chemical process turns into pure single-crystal cylinders four to six inches in diameter which are sliced into wafers or chips.

computing intelligence that could be squeezed onto a silicon wafer has quadrupled. In 1983 the microchip storage capacity was 260,000 pieces of information. By 1984 it was one million pieces of information.

Another example of what is at stake involves computers that are alive, which brings to mind the Englishman Alan Turing's conundrum: put a computer in one room and a human being in a separate room and through an intermediary ask questions of them both. If the intermediary cannot tell which is which solely by their answers, the computer is intelligent.

In this example the 'intelligence' is as much protein as its programmers. The idea of a living, breathing computer is not new but up until now it has not been feasible.

The device resembles other computer boxes which contain silicon microchips on green plastic boards but inside this particular box are extremely thin films of glass covered by invisible layers of protein which constitute a latticework of organic molecules called biochips that quiver at the touch of an electrical current twisting one way or another passing hydrogen atoms as they change positions or shapes. The molecules transmit information in the manner of ordinary integrated circuits but because they are so close together and so small they can perform calculations in roughly a millionth of the time of the most advanced mechanically manufactured chips. The protein transmitters are simple E. coli bacteria organized to perform as chips by genetic engineering, and although the idea seems straight out of science fiction, it is well on the way.

Growing computer circuitry in biology laboratories from living bacteria will relegate the advanced 256K RAM chip with its 262,144 bits of retrieval information to the computer equivalent of the Bronze Age.

A bacterial micro-processor with ten million times the memory of the most advanced current computers *will store all the knowledge ever recorded by man in a desk-top box*. It is presently being developed in the US by physicists, mathematicians, genetic engineers and nuclear biologists and provides an answer to what has been troubling conventional computer engineers and producers: traditional semi-conductor technology has almost reached the limit of memory and miniaturization as more and more information is squeezed onto chips made of silicon. Organic computers offer seemingly unlimited opportunities. They can for example detect inherent flaws and correct them in the same way that – if it were possible – human beings would be able to monitor their own physical ailments and cure them; they can 'heal' and replicate themselves. A large one would be about the size of a hand-held calculator with the memory capacity of a trillion words. A small one would be so minute it could be implanted into a bloodstream to monitor body chemistry, signal processes to correct imbalances and pass along without even creating a heart murmur.

Robots equipped with these supercomputer intelligences could perform better than the most skilled bomber pilots or battle-seasoned foot soldiers.

One of the most knowledgeable people in this field is James McAlear, President of Gentronix Laboratories in Maryland. He is of the opinion that, 'Organic materials will be smaller, faster and cheaper than the increasingly sophisticated equipment needed to etch smaller lines onto conventional chips.' And, 'Because proteins have the ability to assemble themselves, the computer could more or less put itself together.' All that is required is the knowledge of how to programme the bacteria, and that is known.

Scientists in the US and at Warwick University in Britain have been experimenting for some time with organically developed materials that switch on and off like transistors and possess the electrical properties of silicon.

In 1982, when Forrest Carter of the US Naval Research Laboratory anticipated the time when, because computer circuits were getting smaller and smaller, they would ultimately approach the size of molecules, he asked, 'Wouldn't it make more sense to use the molecules themselves?'

From that time forward the experimental work has gone steadily ahead. Carter's vision was of a computer one cubic centimetre (0.061 cubic inch) in size with ten million times the memory capacity of present computers. Granting that what is being discussed here exists on the dual plain of hypothesis and reality, step-by-step development has thus far encountered no obstacles scientists and engineers have not been able to resolve, and the ultimately assured success will without doubt result in a revolution of unprecedented magnitude in an industry which in itself is revolutionary.

And of course Soviet shoppers will appear because biochip technology offers the first-ever view of an absolutely unlimited computer technology. Also, although USSR technology in other fields has achieved parity with the West, in this particular area there is no evidence that it has as yet even got off the ground. That may have something to do with their present and obvious anxiety about the free-world's ability to leave them far behind.

If warfare robotics were enhanced with the new technology with its potential IQ of genius, the possibility of those fifty thousand battle-tanks being able to hold their own against more mobile, infinitely more numerous, smaller, cheaper, easier and faster-to-produce robots would not be encouraging.

Also, a remark made in June 1984 by an official of the Colorado company that manufactures those armed Prowler robots to the effect that there would '... always be a human required in the loop for activation' is evidence of how rapidly things change in the field of electronics. Superchip systems with enormously enhanced 'intelligence', whereby one computer monitors the behaviour and function of another computer, do not require human controls.

Incidentally they can also provide unemotional response – something human intelligence cannot do.

What these recent and impending technological advances mean to the Soviet Union is continuing justification for the existence of the largest and most voracious Intelligence system the world has ever known, and it will agitate an internal situation which has been approaching crisis dimensions for some time. In its simplest form it is called 'change'. In the USSR it impinges upon a particular ambivalence.

In the West there exists a separation between Church and State. In the Soviet Union the division is between the military sector and the civilian.

After the US the Soviet Union has the world's largest annual economy: $1.7 trillion. It was once controlled exclusively by the Party. Currently it is controlled by the military, and suppression supported by the force of law has deprived the civil sector of a growth factor which has inevitably encouraged a stagnating economy; neither protesting nor pointing to a need for redressing the imbalance has been encouraged. Both the Party and the military are inflexibly doctrinaire, opposed to change even while appearing otherwise, as during the arms limitations talks with the West, but there is an increasingly prevailing condition which can bring change.

As Hitler believed he could outrage two-thirds of humanity and win, the Soviets seemed convinced that they can ignore the momentum of progress. But progress does not favour systems or ideologies, only the irreversible force of change. That is where the ambivalence appears.

The Russians spend more money acquiring free-world technology than they spend to support their medical and biological research facilities. This technology is delivered to the military. It is operated by ordinary Russians who as trained specialists inevitably become knowledgeable about such things as computers, telecommunications and the worldwide spread of information.

Party and military policies of restriction and denial may indeed inhibit any general knowledge of these sources of information but they must fail at controlling the personal interest of thousands of Russians who for the first time have access to a means of learning more about the outside world than their forefathers learned.

Ambivalently then, the Soviet drive to acquire advanced foreign technology has imported equipment which has the potential to undermine the political system more success-fully than did Hitler with 120 divisions in 1942, and Soviet authorities have come to realize this fact and to fear it.

For example, Cybernetics, the science of communication and control of machines through computers, has lacked State support for many years because Josef Stalin distrusted it. But Stalin died more than thirty years ago. Since then, partly as a result of programmes to develop indigenous talent and partly as a result of acquisitions from the free-world, Soviet knowledge has increased immensely.

Two particular Russians of note, Yevgeny Velikov, Vice-president of the USSR Academy of Science, and his superior, President Anatoly Alexandrov, have been especially tireless in their drive to encourage automation – robotics – as well as computer technology. Alexandrov said, 'We are failing to make sufficient use of the small amount of computer equipment which is being manufactured here by industry.'

How correct this statement was and also how entrenched is the fear of it is exemplified by the Soviet airline Aeroflot. In London and Washington Aeroflot offices regularly use computers to handle flight data. In Moscow Aeroflot employees use scissors and pens to process the same kind of data.

Another example would be a statement by a Ministry of Education official who said, 'We want our children to do their arithmetic correctly before we hand them calculators. Then we want to know what benefit we will get by widespread introduction to computers.' This statement is axiomatically justifiable but not for the right reasons, although as a means of reflecting State policy is it flawless. As a matter of fact, there would be no 'widespread' use of computers because it is against the law to own one. They fall into the category which prohibits private ownership of copying machines and printing presses – anything which could contribute to dissemination of uncontrolled information.

It amounts to a *Catch 22* situation. The Russian drive to acquire advanced technology is based on the Soviet need to surpass the West, and it is wholeheartedly supported by Party and military leaders. At the same time the advanced technology which is appearing in the country has a great potential to force changes neither the Party nor the military could survive intact.

Soviet leaders allocate a minimum of twenty per cent of the annual national income to obtain free-world technology which they restrict but the Russian technicians who programme computers to calculate the paths of missiles know they can do much more. These are the same knowledgeable individuals who have developed a weather-related data-processing system with military capability and traffic-control points covering the country from Khabarovsk near the Pacific Ocean to Minsk on the Baltic Sea. This system is superior to what is available elsewhere. They are the same Russians who know that computers can 'talk' to other computers and enter foreign computer communication systems to extract information.

But despite this condition which will inevitably impose change, the possibility of its occurring soon is unlikely, and meanwhile, with the military in charge of funding and allocations, even if it were not against Soviet law for unauthorized persons to operate computers, there could be no widespread use because there is no money available to the civil sector for their purchase.

Meanwhile that large slice of the national income which has been allocated for military-related fields has underwritten some projects that are so secret even Intelligence sources can do no better than acquire incomplete information about them.

By way of prefacing what follows, it may be helpful to define the ionosphere. It is the region of the Earth's atmosphere which extends from approximately sixty to a hundred kilometres (37–62 miles) above the Earth's surface, in which there is a high concentration of free electrons formed as a result of ionizing radiation entering the atmosphere from space. It is the province of pure computerized science. At Earth-level amateur radio-operators occasionally encounter evidence of this vast environment through what they call 'woodpecker', a variety of irregular static picked up on certain radio frequencies.

Exploration of the ionosphere depends heavily upon the computerized high technology Russia's leaders fear, but they are committed. For some time their scientists have been conducting ionospheric experiments on the Kola Peninsula, an area with a huge reservoir, Lake Not, which reaches half-way to the Finnish border. There is an excellent rail system linking the peninsula to the southerly Soviet provinces that border European Russia. There is also a relatively ice-free harbour and a Soviet naval base. The entire area is under heavy security which includes electrified fences, guardposts and vehicle and foot patrols, as well as radar and electronic sensors. Here, electrical 'mirrors' have been positioned between one hundred and two hundred kilometres (62–124 miles) above the Earth, which is very high; conventional radar reaches roughly 1.2 to 2.2 Geiger hertz range by a minimum of fifty per cent.

Classified as part of the Soviet defence system or early warning protection against aerial intrusion, which the system actually is because it overcomes the quasi-optical horizon that limits radar and permits Soviet scientists and technicians to 'see' beyond the points which physically limit radar, enhancement has also provided the Soviets with an additional benefit: artificial reflectors that can 'blind' Western radar systems, meaning that aside from giving notice of intrusion the system can provide perfect cover for Soviet aerial launches of 'first-strike' capability.

What focused Intelligence interest on the Kola Peninsula was an explosion of ammunition at the naval base which was initially attributed to either sabotage or carelessness. It was neither.

At that time almost nothing was known in the West about the Ionosphere Project. What was learned later aroused Western concern: there had been a 'bounce-back' from space which had detonated the ammunition. Using the latest cybernetic technology, Soviet scientists had been experimenting. According to an Intelligence report which did not originate in the US, the Soviets were 'definitely engaged in a weather war'. The same report also stated that '... it is mainly Soviet experiments which ... [have been] ... causing floods, intense cold, and drought conditions, particularly on the African Continent, since 1980.' According to these sources, the Soviets employed the 'standing wave' system of atmospheric interference, the actual results of which can be explained only through theory and whose real and future effects cannot be satisfactorily explained even that way.

Since 1979 major weather-tampering signals have been lofted into the ionosphere on a large scale from the Kola Peninsula. There have been coincidental alterations of weather patterns over a large part of Europe, Siberia and the Middle East. In Africa, where drought is not uncommon, it has increased in duration. Hundreds of thousands of people and animals have died as a result. In Europe there have been unprecedentedly dry summers.

The Kola Peninsula ionosphere experimental installation was such a well-kept secret it even duped surveillance satellites but it was not the only secret Soviet programme which accomplished this. Another was a huge phased-array radar system in south-central Siberia where the receiving and transmitting screens were at least 152.4 metres (500 feet) wide and as tall as a thirty-storey building.

This Abalakova facility had the capability of 'seeing hundreds of targets simultaneously and sending missiles against them. In effect it was a battle station which could function as a supreme headquarters. It had the technology to detect warheads at a great distance, compute such things as trajectory, speed and destination, and deliver this information to battle-management systems for immediate response to incoming projectiles by launching intercepter missiles supported by radar guidance.

It was a system for defence and as such was consistent with provisions of the Anti-Ballistic Missile Treaty. Western Intelligence knew of at least six of these Soviet phased-array radar installations. According to the 1972 Treaty they were to be built on national borders as early-warning systems and were not to be enhanced to become missile-launching sites. However, the Abalakova facility is nowhere near the national border. It is strategically located for launching missiles against US ICBM fields and has been enhanced to accomplish that purpose. Its radar closes the last gap in Soviet defence against ballistic missile approaches while at the same time providing the USSR with an advantageous first-strike capability. It appears to be part of a Soviet network of these facilities masquerading as non-aggressive early-warning radar installations. Because it is unlikely that such a system could have been built and enhanced except over a great many years, quite probably Soviet scientists and engineers were working toward completion of the system while the 1972 Treaty was under discussion.

The facility itself is very large and therefore could not avoid detection by aerial surveillance but it was not the huge radar screens and buildings which were not detected: it was the enhancement, and this was competently hidden from overhead viewing.

This facility uses sophisticated computers as well as other equally advanced technology. It is slanted to make the most of space viewing which is consistent with the Soviet policy to make space of top-priority importance in their strategic planning notwithstanding their current stand against weapons in space. In fact, they developed the first killer satellite in 1971. It was a weapon. Its purpose was to destroy Western reconnaissance satellites. They have also utilized acquired Western technology and their own indigenous scientific talent to develop a formidable 'ABM mode' capable of frightening enhancement and forbidden by the 1972 Treaty.

The 'ABM Mode' is a complete weapons system which deploys SA-12 missiles or their successors. Its purpose is to destroy missiles or aircraft in space and it is mobile. It has target-tracking radar mounted on the same vehicle that carries the weapons system. SA-12s have the potential of reaching and destroying targets in the US or Europe.

The US developed a similar weapon, the Patriot missile, which could be enhanced to achieve the same capability as the SA-12 but has not been because the 1972 Treaty forbids it.

Defining the extent of the SA-12 system has run head-on into Soviet secrecy and deception, but satellite information suggests that the SA-12 system is extensive. Satellites have photographed a number of mobile units while moving and stationary but, despite their size and the retinue of supporting troops, have been unable to see through the heavy protective camouflage.

Satellites have also photographed thousands of what appear to be industrial buildings, generally too small to house SA-12 units in areas where industrial plants are rare. Analysts suspect these are the above-ground service and support facilities for extensive underground SA-12 installations. If so, the SA-12 weapon system which can be operated in conjunction with phased-array radar stations provides such sites as the Abalakova facility with a complete ABM system.

13
The Borderland

A rather general knowledge of high technology, what it may portend and the efforts of the Russians to acquire it, has been around for years – ordinarily without particularization except to record the details of spy-hunts, rarely with enough objectivity to provide a balanced view of what has been acquired and why someone has wanted to acquire it, or what their motivations were, or their methods of acquisition, subjects which are essential to an understanding of what effect these things will have on the future.

Robots, for example, are not new. Robotics were of interest forty years ago. But generally little has been known about their limitations or their physical structure. In terms of proliferation or as weapons, reliable information has been scarce but most importantly the field of robot-enhancement has been a blank page. The robot of forty years ago or even five years ago has little in common with the present generation of robots and even less with robots of the future whose production is close.

Is a sophisticated robot as dangerous to human society as a nuclear device? Yes, because it can 'think'. Unlike biological brains made largely of water and susceptible to deterioration or injury, artificial intelligence does not require fluid, nor can it 'die' or deteriorate. It can age in the sense that newer, more sophisticated models can supersede it but, even if it cannot be enhanced to compete with newer 'brains', it is still usable. It can be injured but it can also be repaired; there is no 'permanent brain damage' nor can it be 'born' retarded or become senile. Like the human brain artificial intelligence in robots or computers uses the force of reason. Biological intelligence thinks through reasoning and training – another term for experience. Artificial intelligence

132

operates in much the same way, only faster, and although computer intelligence is at the stage of development where it can enhance its own programming, it nevertheless remains basically an appliance; it 'reasons' through mathematics, not instinct.

That artificial intelligence can be so enormously improved is because, among other things, the basic steps which underlie mathematics are very simple while they are at the same time capable of achieving limitless intellectual capability.

Two basics make this possible: First, if 1 is a valid number, which of course it is, *and* 2 is another basic number, then adding them together produces the number 3. Artificial intelligence is programmed to accept no other answer. The same with 1,000 million plus 2,000 million or 43½ million added to 98 and 113 million. Artificial intelligence cannot arrive at any response but the correct one. Human intelligence is not that error-free.

The other basic verifies that if 1 is a valid number *or* 2 is valid, then 3 is their total. 'And' as well as 'or' is the code for this reasoning. In biological brains this reasoning process is accomplished by 'gates' where reason and an electrical current meet. In artificial intelligence the 'gates' are made of electronic diodes or transistors. In human brains the 'gates' are neurons, or nerve cells. A 'gate' in either instance is a pathway which opens to permit the passage of electricity to flow when programmed conditions exist so that the correct response will occur.

When somewhat different kinds of 'gates' are added to the artificial intelligence, it is called enhancement. An accumulation of 'gates' will allow an enhanced artificial intelligence to subtract and multiply as well as add. Additional enhancements will enable the intelligence to prepare error-free tax returns, solve problems of higher mathematics or, going farther, 'tell' its host robot which roads to travel to enter a besieged city, when to stop advancing and start killing. It 'knows' how many miles or city blocks to travel, where to turn into particular streets, where to begin the destruction.

Hans Moravec's 'stupid' robot is the one programmed to do just one thing. It cannot depart from its repertoire. It has a lot in common with animals and insects. It will react stupidly in a novel situation. It is an unintelligent robot with an unintelligent computer brain. It is ideal for unsophisticated military use. But it can probably be enhanced to perform multiple operations. And if the Amdahl superchip is available and is interchangeable with the 'stupid' program which operates the robot, the only requirement is for a computer technician to insert a new program into the robot's computer memory. It automatically erases the previous memory and takes command, and the robot responds by accomplishing more sophisticated – or deadly – functions.

If a human being burns his finger, reason based upon painful experience tells him not to put his finger into the fire again. His reason comes from painful memory. Artificial reasoning works the same way except that there is no pain. There is instead a heat sensor to 'tell' the brain not to repeat the operation.

Hang the sensors, or chips, together, and the more that are used the more the system is improved. Or, with a superchip, there is more memory – 'intelligence' – and faster response time. Put into another context, if an enemy hits a robot with an incendiary projectile, the robot moves away quickly, as a soldier would, but the soldier would probably require medical attention and the robot would probably survive the scorching and remain operable.

High technology takes many forms. Computer 'intelligence' serves nearly all of them. Improvements appear more quickly than the passing seasons, and each improvement is vital to some particular system, tanks, missiles, robots, aircraft, warships, ionospheric experiments, telecommunications, even writing, and therefore the Soviet pursuit has had to become faster. It has also become more difficult, and will no doubt become even more so, as Western security measures improve, but the need to acquire high-tech will increase accordingly. That means clandestine suppliers will have to take greater risks, but in compensation, the financial rewards will be greater. In special cases they are already quite spectacular.

In the West the free societies seem to consider continued advanced development its own rewards. Without the same sense of urgency, except to see who can create the best superchip, free societies have been so engrossed in their own race they have neglected the other race, the one that views all technology in terms of military use.

Members of the free societies who profess altruism as their motivation for denouncing censorship, even assuming that their altruism is genuine, as well as others whose sincerity is more questionable, share a blind spot. In the Soviet Union a paralleling quandary which comes from fear of the things which have been acquired seems to arise from a similar disinclination to accept reality, and both are at the mercy of successive tidal waves of technology and the certain changes and responsibilities they carry with them.

At least the Soviet Union has an entrenched ideology. Stridently different points of view have never caused the same degree of disarray in Russia they have in the West, where ideology has not united people effectively since the days of National Socialist Germany.

Soviet intransigence remains steadfast although ambiguous. The most recent example of this may be found in the current Soviet refusal to discuss weapons in space which appears to be the result of pique over the positioning of US missiles in Europe. This may be the excuse for intransigence, not the cause of it. The Ionosphere Project and other secret experimental programmes with equally as terrible implications may be the cause – they, and the unyielding dogma of Soviet officials, the same dogma which continues to push military power beyond the nation's defensive needs, and meanwhile the rummaging continues, while behind it, Soviet marshals feed the war machine and see spectres everywhere. When they recently warned East Germans about keeping their distance from West Germans, Party newspapers in Hungary as well as in East Germany protested editorially on the grounds that co-operation was doing a service 'to both Europe and the world'. China and Japan are considered American allies by the Kremlin leaders. Poland is a political quagmire even as Afghanistan has proved to be a military one.

The need to obtain ever-better technology also stems from Russia's fears about its borders. As political winds shift, the historic paranoia has become an obsession. The nation's vast arsenal has been used more frequently against its own citizens and its allies than against others. It struggles to prevent all varieties of advanced technology from spreading within its borders while keeping armies of agents abroad to buy or steal technology, which is brought into the country. Russia has become a borderland, an ambivalent giant with a foot on both sides. Its best years were the 1960s and 1970s, when its arch-enemy, the United States, was weakened by a war in south-east Asia, the internal political crisis of the Watergate scandal and diminishing military power. Simultaneously there was a softening of NATO determination, disagreement and confusion in Europe where the line should be drawn to halt Soviet expansionism, and economic trouble.

Since then the Soviet agricultural sector has failed so dismally to feed the nation that funds allocated to other sectors, even to some extent the military, have had to be re-routed for the purchase from overseas sources of grain (6.8 million tons from the US in July 1984), meat, even butter. And there is a stagnating economy having trouble supporting Russia's end of the arms race, including the expense of high-tech acquisition.

Even uprisings in the Third World, largely stimulated by Russia, have been more of a drain than a benefit. The country can digest just so much Cuban sugar. But fortunately for the Soviets one of the lulls which ordinarily occur in the course of empire-building now obtains, and into the foreseeable future relatively inexpensive entrenchment can replace the earlier strident adventurism. But those who see the current *diminuendo* as disarray or loss of vigour resulting from economic doldrums would do better to appreciate that, although Soviet goals appear to have been moderated because of ailing prospects at home and less need for pushing them elsewhere, they have been neither moderated nor abandoned: they have simply become less tactical and more strategic.

For example, where possible, trade-offs have been used to alleviate the financial drain. The Soviets offered $200 million worth of missiles to Kuwait and agreed to buy $200 million worth of Saudi-Arabian oil, which amounts to a checkmate and two diplomatic advantages, cost free. In the Middle East the Soviets signed a treaty with Egypt to resume diplomatic relations, which put Soviet agents back where they have not been for a decade, another inexpensive triumph, and they are presently advocating an Arab-Israeli peace settlement to divert attention from a quiet and inexpensive incursion in Lebanon where even ports and barracks do not have to be built, having already been established by other outsiders.

Objectives have not changed, only the means for obtaining them, partly out of necessity and partly because of the lull which requires the use of strategy in place of tactics. Nor has anything been lost, and a fringe benefit is that the money saved can be re-allocated to the military. There too, judicious spending prevails. Money can be saved on tank, truck and aircraft fuel by using poison gas, which is cheap. And developing robotics in order to produce armies of killer robots would amount to a considerable saving over tank production. Support of Iraq in its war with Iran could be a very cheap way to achieve Soviet presence and influence in the region of Middle Eastern oil production. Nor is the strategy here without additional significance, because even if the Iranians win their war against Iraq, as proclaimed enemies of the Saudis, with Iraq defeated, Iran's irresponsible leaders could sweep across the sand with nothing to stop them – except a more powerful Soviet presence. The Saudis, formerly enemies of Russia and friends of the US, have already begun their fence-mending.

Inexpensive strategy could accomplish in the Persian Gulf periphery what sixty months of expensive warfare has been unable to accomplish in Afghanistan. From this 'little war' may have arisen leadership fissures at the Soviet top level, or so indications seem to suggest, but not in the nature of the power struggles of the past, rather over costs in comparison to benefits. If the economy could pull free of its present slump, that contentiousness would no doubt vanish. Whether it does or not, erosion elsewhere could continue, particularly in two areas, those of acquisition, which provides the USSR with Western high technology, and control.

Physical control should not be difficult in a country which has more policemen than all Europe combined, but physical control has not been a problem in the USSR, while aberrant ideologies have been, and inevitably they will continue to be. It seems to be only a matter of time before artificial intelligence, so sophisticated and commonplace elsewhere, will appear. Control of computers and of telecommunication links, both those inside the country and those beyond which are piling up along the Soviet-European borderlands, could become an impossible task.

How long will it be before those free-world disseminators of the information which is beamed over the air-waves into Soviet Russia combine their talents with those who produce low-cost electronic pen-sized calculators for schoolchildren to produce millions of Russian-speaking little computerized 'pencils' to be surreptitiously passed from hand to hand? How does a police state control something as pervading as information which intrudes from all sides simultaneously? How are the pacification troops outside the country to be protected against the information which is at the root of Russia's present soaring rate of defection?

Russia is a borderland where control on one side is threatened by lack of control on the other side, and what a war might not be able to accomplish, if the floodgates were ever breached, might be accomplished – not swiftly and not without sacrifice, but accomplished nonetheless – as a result of the Age of Information.

The quandary has increased as the variations and sophistication of electronic communications have proliferated. For the Soviet Union the perils are far greater than if the nation were threatened by hostile armed might. For the West, where lack of an appreciation of *realpolitik* has prevailed for a half century, the peril is equally as clear but as the progeny of different parents.

The central problem was defined by a believer in open societies: 'Ours is a free state both in politics and daily life – we are superior to our enemies ... our city is open to the world. We are not always expelling foreigners for fear of their learning or seeing something of military importance. We live freely and yet we face the same dangers as readily as they ...' The speaker was Pericles of Athens who died in 429 BC and whose ideal society was entombed by the might of a militarist state, Sparta, having survived for fourteen years. Perhaps historians will one day judge whether Athens fell because it was a free society which allowed spies to operate unhindered, as they make a similar judgement about more contemporary free societies.

The substance of this difference may be, as philosophers have often said, that 'Victory is on the side of the patient.' Unfortunately there have been enough examples to the contrary in the history of nations, beginning with Pericles' Athens, to cast a little doubt.

For the West the problem seems to be the inability to recognize the dangers, or weaknesses, of free societies and try to achieve a balance between freedom and security. For the Soviets, who are forced to have a foot on both sides of all the borders as long as they must keep pace with their adversaries, it is unlikely any Spartans will appear in armour carrying spears, but it is equally unlikely that, providing that in emulation of the enraged scorpion they do not sting themselves into oblivion by launching a war, they will be able to prevent the technological advances loose in the free-world from penetrating their best barriers in many forms, but most damaging to their hierarchies and their system in the forms of factual, balanced information, the kind a computer can project on its 'screen' for hours on end, with texts, diagrams and statistics. How much time would be required to tabulate by name the ten million Ukrainians Josef Stalin allegedly killed? Would it be difficult for such information to gain access to the Soviet Union? No. Granting the existence of very strong controls and the certainty of their enhancement as the danger increases, the same element which has enabled the USSR to become the most formidable aggressive military power in the world at the present time, ideas, and their lack of susceptibility to controls, guarantees that penetration will occur. How and when are matters of conjecture. Closed societies, police states, realms of secrecy have never been simple targets. But in all history penetration has never before had electronic sophistication to support it of the kind which has also supported the ability to alter the weather, to produce artificial intelligence and to transmit reams of information at the speed of light.

The unfortunate aspect of all this is that old mentalities rule the Soviet Union's segment of a new world. A pointless hypothesis is that, granted an opportunity to change, would the Russians take it? More relevant is the question: whether they would or not, what will the Soviet leadership feel impelled to recognize as their necessary course of action, now, because clearly the Soviet borderland is at an historic crossroad: war may or may not end with the establishment of a worldwide Slavic empire, but it will certainly end with human existence no longer moving ahead as it now is, toward some awesome and incredible thresholds in knowledge, time and space. Any number of seer-sciences suggest answers but only one has a correct answer and the KGB would concur: on-site espionage.

In mid-August 1984 a British magazine, *Jane's Defence Weekly*, published photographs of construction at the Nikolayev 444 shipyard on the Black Sea of a nuclear-powered aircraft-carrier, tentatively named the *Kremlin*. Nothing exemplifies better both the military's domination of the nation and the policy which will be pursued in the future by Soviet leaders.

The *Kremlin* dramatizes Russia's fifteen-year passage from a coast-defence naval force to a sea-going power of global importance. The *Kremlin* is to be one of eight proposed nuclear-powered aircraft-carriers. It will displace something like 70,000 tons, equal to the displacement of the smallest US carrier. (The largest US aircraft-carriers displace 91,500 tons.) The *Kremlin* will not be ready for shake-down trials until 1988. It will carry sixty aircraft. (Large US carriers accommodate up to ninety aircraft.) It will measure 1,105 feet in length, making it the longest fighting ship in the world. The proposed complement of aircraft will be MiG 23 fighters, new Su-27 flanker counter-air fighters and advanced early-warning electronic-surveillance aircraft.

The *Kremlin* reflects Soviet determination to increase Russian might. This is further supported by Soviet fleet Admiral Sergei Gorshkov's orders to establish a construction record for naval shipyards in completing the *Kremlin* ahead of projections.

The objective of aircraft-carriers is to provide aerial

protection to naval forces engaged beyond the range of land-based fighter aircraft and to support troops engaged on land beyond the range of airfields.

For years the USSR has operated conventional-powered, small aircraft-carriers that carry helicopters and vertical-take-off 'jump-jet' fighters, and they are still building them, but with the advent of the *Kremlin* and eight more like it to follow, as *Jane's* magazine said, there will now be '... potentially formidable adversaries for the US Navy's carrier-battle groups'.

Obviously, economic shortfalls in recent times have created problems even in the military sector, but equally obviously they have not been allowed to interfere in areas which impinge upon foreign policy. The USSR does not need large aircraft-carriers. However, any aggressive power does require support systems for ground forces it anticipates using beyond its borders. The USSR has the ground forces, and its foreign policy certainly anticipates using them, therefore aircraft-carrying support systems must be produced.

If, as Russian rhetoric has professed for years, the nation only wants to be able to defend itself, then it does not need aircraft-carriers, and Bismarck's dictum about the bayonets (page 9) gains additional significance. If there were ambiguities, who in the Soviet Union would mention them? But that does not mean they do not exist. It simply means they must remain in the secret heart of those who have them, until eventually that tide of intelligence upon the free side of the borderland is able to seep through to encourage questioning people to find others who also have doubts about policies which imperil all life while draining the national wealth to create an enormous war machine, the same policies that allocate resources to build apartment warrens of inferior quality and less than a third as many as the population requires; the same policies which have perpetuated the historic fears Russians have always lived with, that enemies are everywhere, that their borders are sieves through which hostile hordes may appear at any moment.

They have appeared. Russian history is a story of invasion, bloodshed and subjugation. But that was when Russia was a divided land. That was Russia, not the Soviet Union. Now,

'Russia' is the land-mass, the nation is the Soviet Union, a united country. There are no longer the relevant comparisons. Only one neighbour, China, can approach the USSR in size. Otherwise all the old enemies have been swept into the dustbin of history, and some have disappeared altogether. But China is not really, tactically, the threat Soviet propagandists repeatedly warn their countrymen it is. What Napoleon said about the overwhelming mass of Chinese armies constituting a threat to Europe – that they do not have to be feared because they are such poor swimmers – is relevant here. Numbers would not make the difference. What the outnumbered Germans did to the Russians at Tannenberg in 1914, the Soviets could do to the Chinese now. True, China has the atom bomb. The Soviets possess an arsenal of such vastly more lethal capability that there cannot really be a comparison of offensive power. The greatest armed host of history opposing one of the poorest armed hosts implies a terrible but one-sided contest.

But the old mentalities in the Kremlin, who know first-hand what a strong enemy can accomplish, live with that memory. Also, they have political reasons for keeping Russians convinced of the peril. In most World War II nations the past has not been buried but it has not been kept alive either. In the USSR battles such as Stalingrad are celebrated as though they occurred yesterday. It is necessary to keep them alive because nothing unites a people as profoundly as what they have survived, and what they believe may happen again. What other possible excuse can be used to justify a military build-up so huge and expensive that it absorbs resources the way a sponge absorbs water? Even to whisper doubts is unheard-of. But they do exist, and to counter them nothing serves Party purposes better than keeping the old fears alive.

In the USSR re-affirming the faithful and proselytizing are major functions of Party ideologues. Since 1956, when the Cominform was dissolved, there has been no single Soviet agency which directs all the operations of international Communism. But under the Central Committee those duties have been an essential part of Soviet internal and external policy.

However, in fact, the continuing façade while essential to internal control now exists as the cover for pure militarism.

Even abroad in some client states such as Cuba, two levels exist, one of cynicism, one of belief. Belief is kept thriving by the ideologues, by inflationary but busy economies, by providing manufactured threats from the outside and by physical controls. The cynics, with little reason to fear interference as long as the ideologues do their work, are free to create their juggernaut. And they have created it.

In summary, what the American psych-ware (psychological-software) salesman James Johnson developed for the narrow fields of psychiatry and business, Soviet 'salesmen' have perfected over the years for a broader spectrum of use in roughly the same categories: how to control and manipulate people, millions of them; how to classify human beings for exploitation, and, going James Johnson one better, how to maintain that level of manipulation for generations.

None of this offers much in the way of startling revelations. It simply confirms that few changes have occurred. What it may do is direct attention to what has been the result of no-change: policies which have expanded, technologies which have improved, systems which have achieved sophistication, and goals which have passed through periods of sharp refinements to more clearly defined ideas and ambitions which, because of anachronism, lack of relevance to current, modern, advanced civilization, are dangerous.

The Soviet system, led by old minds, reached its optimum and passed it. What opportunities it once had were tailored to a world of something like $1\frac{1}{2}$ billion human beings, most of whom had neither rights or freedom. They achieved those things not in a single case through Soviet assistance, as they increased in numbers to three billion people, and during that time and to the present Soviet interference did not promote freedom or dignity: it agitated instead for the opposite of both, still promoting intellectual sterility and outmoded dogmatism, its leaders men with minds locked into a period, and a system dominated by hypothesists who were never more than ubiquitous pests. Unobservant, blind ones at that. Soviet leaders make the identical errors earlier despots made. They bend every resource to create a pyramid of armour they cannot see over. Upon the far side is the three-quarters of the world they have antagonized, and no system yet has been able to overcome those odds, not even, as in Hitler's case, when it had more and better arms and soldiers than anyone else had.

But triumph is not the issue. Hitler lacked warheads, lasers, an experienced overseas espionage apparatus (he had none in fact, except for a few bunglers). He lacked a twenty-year accumulation of armament which included a genuine navy. He could not wage anything but limited warfare. His air force equalled that of Britain but not that of America. He embarked upon an advanture without proper planning and edequate force. He could be defeated. His generals knew it when war began.

Soviet leaders have planned well, have had the time to create their pyramid and continue to have the time to add to it almost as though by tonnage alone they wish to smother the free-world. But that is not the issue either.

It is that they are willing to start a war. Worse, they are willing to do so in support of outdated convictions which even in victory they could not sustain.

The basis of their entire system is control, destruction of free initiative; in its place subjugation to the flawed ideology. But an incinerated world would not need controls–for either side. At ground-level gassed populaces and poisoned soil would result in a great, contamminated void of silence, no machinery turning, no people requiring either good or bad leadership, no birds, no animals, no people to read or write or reach into the cosmos, to unbutton the sequence of physics and genetics which presently seem close to providing a number of incredible answers.

For what purpose? To achieve the goal of a Red world? All that vast armament does not guarantee it can be achieved. Even the effort to achieve it would require a sacrifice to the point of exhaustion for a system that could not survive a proliferation of the maggots inherent in its own body. The captive states would certainly break away. Some, like Poland, would require armies of occupation. Others, the Soviet 'Autonomous Republics', such as the Ukraine where even the slaughter of ten million people has not resulted in extinguishing the embers of revolt, require only a reasonable hope of success to opt for separation. Let the system become extended, weakened, and disintegration will begin. That is not a theory: it is a lesson from history, a fact of strife.

Certainly the old minds have considered the risks and the costs. Of the costs they could reflect some of Josef Stalin's indifference. They demonstrated this most recently by approval of cruelty in Afghanistan. A man for whom a famous thoroughfare was named in Moscow, Maxim Gorky (otherwise Peshkov), said that, 'Cruelty is the characteristic of the Russian people.'

As for the risks, for no other reason than to minimize them during the pursuit of conquest has that huge accumulation of military hardware been stockpiled. To minimize them, not to avoid them. There exists a feudal view of life beneath the onion domes. Goals are important, life never is. Disposal is a routine, uncomplicated affair, requiring routine, uncomplicated solutions.

For example, as early as October 1980 it was known in Intelligence circles that Pope John Paul II would arrive in Poland for the second time during the second week of June 1981. His earlier visit had been significant for the founding of the Solidarity Movement, widespread civil disorder and near open rebellion against Soviet hegemony. The problem for Soviet overlords arose not only from Polish affection for the first-ever Polish pope; there were 700 million Catholics in the world. As a threat John Paul could not be denigrated; neither could the puppet government of Poland refuse to allow his visit. Either course would almost certainly result in an uprising in Poland and 700 million sympathizers elsewhere. The Pope could not be allowed to visit Poland, and he could not be refused the right to visit Poland.

One month after it was learned that John Paul intended to enter Poland, in November 1980, a secret meeting of Warsaw Pact Intelligence services was convened in Bucharest – from which Polish Intelligence delegates were excluded. On the agenda for discussion was the upcoming papal visit. In attendance at the meeting was Soviet Minister of Defence Marshal Dmitry F. Ustinov, at that time the most powerful man in the USSR. Cutting through the dissemblers, Marshal Ustinov proposed assassination as the simplest means for preventing the papal visit. He had a name for the undertaking: 'the Rasputin Project'.* The rest is history. If someone of Ustinov's prestige would journey to Bucharest, the reason had to be vitally important. That he proposed assassination reflects the almost primitive viewpoint of Soviet leaders. It was far from being the only alternative.

If a renowned holy man could be so off-handedly sentenced to death, of what value would other human life be which exists as a threat only because it is there?

How intransigent are those old minds? Professional negotiators in London and Washington have never abandoned hope. They are largely responsible for creating the Soviet war machine by adhering to a policy Stalin ridiculed: achieve understanding and friendship by appeasement. Supply the Soviet Union with loans, technicians, even complete factories. Provide advanced technology, make excuses for Russian abuses and excesses. Keep talking, wheedling, yielding, giving. Accept one concession out of three, which leaves the USSR with two intact, blind to what the results of this policy has ensured. Enter into secret treaties – as President Kennedy did with the Soviets to get the missiles out of Cuba – be indulgent of Soviet espionage in the free-world. The old minds will not change. They came to power because they would not change. They will support KGB programmes and military aims for the same reason. Of course they are not immortal, as Andropov and Chernenko proved, but the question this poses is: will their successors be more moderate?

There is no answer but to wait. Meanwhile it is the old minds and their view of the world which matter. They have, as quite likely their successors will also have, the desire to retain power. In a rigidly closed society promotion comes through obedience to whatever has ensured the continuity of strength and power.

If it were possible to believe, as the negotiators have

---

* As a matter of interest, the East German delegate responded favourably. The Hungarian and Romanian delegates demurred.

believed, that change in leadership broadens prospects for changes in policy, then time might be an ally of the patient. In the Soviet Union there have been five changes since Stalin. Nothing has changed except the momentum to reach a goal of military superiority.

Presently, that zenith has been reached, in some categories surpassed. What remains as a ponderable is the free-world's ability to spring a surprise, as was hinted at in President Reagan's spring of 1983 address – called by the media his 'Star Wars' talk – in which it was said that the solution to missile attack might be an electronic 'shield' reaching from ground-level to the ionosphere, an idea that puts pressure on Soviet shoppers to locate laboratories where such a programme of development may be in progress, because if it is, and the Soviets cannot obtain it, the implications are serious. A deterrent screen able to thwart very heavy intercontinental missiles should have no difficulty thwarting artillery shells, possibly bomber overflights, even conventional bullets.

That could indeed result in someone owning a very large scrap pile in a very large borderland.

14
Pericles' Athens Revisited

In 1983 the US increased the tempo of its dialogues with the USSR on a variety of subjects. It, and its allies, met with Soviet delegates in Washington, Moscow, Geneva, Vienna and Madrid. Chief representatives were US Secretary of State George Schultz and Soviet Ambassador Dobrynin. The range of discussions was rather comprehensive: arms control, human rights, regional developments, bilateral issues involving trade and exchanges. In the summer '83 round of strategic arms reduction and balanced force reduction talks (START), Soviet negotiators cast forth a few small pearls. They allowed some religious families to leave the Soviet Union who had been living in sanctuary within the US Embassy at Moscow for several years. They also signed a long-term grain-purchase agreement. An additional gain was an agreement by the Soviet Union to discuss improving the US-Soviet hot-line and other crisis communication systems, and agreement eventually to discuss cultural exchanges and the establishment of new consulates in both countries.

The world Press took heart by reporting a warming trend between the West and Russia. Moderation was in the air. The era of no-change was perhaps ending. By late August 1983 a scheduled meeting between Soviet Foreign Minister Gromyko* and Secretary of State Schultz at the concluding session of the Madrid Conference on Security and Co-operation in Europe (CSCE) was to augment agreements and inaugurate an era of co-operation.

On 31 August Soviet air defence forces shot down Korea

---

* Nikita Khrushchev once said that if he told Gromyko 'to take down his pants and sit on a cake of ice' until told to arise, he would do so.

Air Lines Flight 007 with 269 civilian passengers aboard, as the KAL aircraft was leaving Soviet air space over Sakhalin Island above the Sea of Japan. In the ensuing uproar several unique inconsistencies emerged. One of the last passengers aboard was US Congressman Lawrence Patton McDonald, a conservative Democrat from Georgia who was also head of the fiercely anti-Communist Western Goals Foundation, an expanding, well-funded organization with offices in Washington, France and West Germany. At the time of the KAL 007 incident Western Goals Foundation was preparing to publicize in detail an exposé of the large underground espionage and acquisition network created in West Germany by Soviet Ambassador Vladimir Seminov. Congressman McDonald was on his way to Seoul for talks with Korean Air Marshal Chang Chi Ryang. It was Chang Chi Ryang who, while Korean ambassador to Denmark, established monitoring stations in Scandinavia to oversee Soviet sea traffic in Scandinavian waters. He accomplished this through one of the most experienced anti-Communist agents in Scandinavia*.

Earlier, in April 1978, a KAL Boeing 747 aeroplane strayed off course and was crippled by gunfire from a Soviet warplane and forced to land on a frozen lake with two dead passengers. At that time Soviet authorities said they tracked the aircraft for two hours and fired tracers across its bow as a signal to land. The KAL pilot, Captain Kim Chang Kyu, a veteran commercial pilot, said he saw a Soviet warplane, signalled it by reducing speed and, using landing lights, gave the international signals that he would follow the interceptor to a landing site. Without warning the warplane fired a missile which sheared off fourteen feet of the airliner's left wing, holed the fuselage and killed two passengers. Captain Kim was able to make a successful forced landing. He and his passengers were imprisoned.

When Ambassador Chang Chi Ryang, who is a tough, no-nonsense individual, met the Soviet ambassador in Denmark, he said, 'You and I know you were testing equipment for throwing navigational instruments off

---

* At this writing living incognito in Fort Lauderdale, Florida.

course. You chose us, as a warning, to cease certain operations. We are not interfering with your operations and we are not going to stop ours. You are going to release the passengers and crew and I am not going to say anything and neither will you.' The crew and passengers were released and Air Marshal Chang Chi Ryang kept them away from the Press until they reached Seoul.

Were Air Marshal Chang's statements true? The KAL aeroplane was a thousand miles off course in one of the most sensitive areas of the USSR where there were secret missile sites, large naval perimeters, advanced electronic installations and numerous air bases. Also, there were about 2,500 interceptor aircraft and as many as 10,000 SAM missiles, part of the Soviet Air Defence Forces (*Voiska Protivovozdushnoi Oborony*) whose responsibility is to guard the nation's borders. Air defence radar was competent and advanced. The Korean airliner flew for two hours through this area and was not challenged in all that time until it was turning away. Then it was attacked and forced to land.

In the second incident, that of KAL Flight 007, explanations of the tragedy implied a 'navigational error' by Captain Chun Byung In who, at forty-five years of age, had 10,000 hours in the air with 6,618 of them in Boeing 747s. If there was a navigational error, Captain Chun evidently did not know it. In his last report monitored in Tokyo he said his position was 113 miles south-east of Hokkaido. He was in fact 113 miles *north* of Hokkaido, heading toward the Soviet island of Sakhalin from the tip of Kamchatka Peninsula where the Soviets have their highly restricted Petropavlovsk missile, naval and submarine base, and beyond which are the Soviet Kuril Islands where intense military activity has been in progress for several years. His normal route would have been a gradual, large curve from Anchorage, Alaska, out to sea well beyond Kamchatka and the Kurils. He would have been nowhere near Sakhalin Island. But in fact his actual route took him over the Sakhalin naval base at Korsakov – near which he was shot down – and would have had him skirt close to the mainland Russian Sovietskaya Gavan air and naval base and either over or very close to Vladivostok, headquarters of the Soviet Pacific Fleet.

If it had been Captain Chun's intention to violate Soviet airspace, he could not have picked a worse place to do it, which he certainly would have known. He had flown the North Pacific (NORPAC) route from Anchorage to Seoul for five years, in 1982 was cited for an accident-free record and as a former colonel in the South Korean Air Force knew that no intruding aircraft could over-fly this particular Soviet territory without being attacked.

If it was not his intention, had this veteran pilot made a navigational error? Boeing 747s are equipped with three of the best navigational systems known. They are accurate in electrical storms and despite *conventional* radio interference. Because KAL flights which skirt restricted Soviet zones also carry additional navigational aids, pilot error would be unlikely but to eliminate even that possibility KAL standard procedure required extensive double-checking by other flight crewmen, and laxness could probably be ruled out because the previous, 1978, Soviet attack on a KAL aircraft was still fresh in the minds of pilots and crewmen.

The inconsistencies began to multiply. For example, although transcripts of Japanese radio-operators who monitored Captain Chun's flight appeared in print almost immediately after the tragedy, not all the conversations were made public and still have not been. Another inconsistency concerned the Soviet denial that they had shot down an airliner, and when eventually they did admit it, their defence was that the KAL 747 was mistaken for a US reconnaissance RC-135 aircraft which had previously been in the area but which had landed at its Aleutian base before Flight 007 was attacked. The lack of resemblance between an RC-135 and a 747 would be obvious even to non-aviators.

Initially it was stated by the Russians that the attacking fighter-pilot did not recognize Flight 007 as a commercial aircraft because of poor visibility. It was also stated that visual contact was made at eight miles and the pilot closed to $1\frac{1}{2}$ miles before aligning his fighter for the kill. A range of $1\frac{1}{2}$ miles is not poor visibility.

Finally, when recriminations, denials and defiance faded and responsibility for the attack was tentatively fixed upon the field officer who ordered the 747 destroyed, Japanese listening-posts cast doubts upon the allegation that no one higher up had anything to do with the attack. During the two hours during which KAL Flight 007 was in Soviet airspace, communications between Sakhalin defence posts and other Soviet military facilities were continuous, and during this time at least four Soviet fighter aircraft were stalking the KAL airliner. Sakhalin defence authorities were in constant contact with Moscow. When the ultimate decision was made to shoot the aeroplane down, the orders came from Moscow not a field officer's command post.

A minutely detailed account of what actually happened might present the physical facts, but fixing responsibility would require something more: an understanding that every Russian who was involved, from the official in Moscow to the field commander who relayed verbal orders for the assault to the Su-15 pilot who fired the missile, behaved exactly in accordance with the requirements of Soviet military procedures as they have been practised by Soviet leaders over the past twenty years.

The law (Article 36, Soviet Border Law) states that weapons are to be employed against 'armed provocation ...', which is interpreted to mean any provocation whether it is accidental or perhaps deliberately caused, as Air Marshal Chang Chi Ryang said of the earlier attack upon a KAL airliner, by technicians experimenting with equipment for 'throwing navigational instruments off course'. Certainly this type of experimental equipment has been tested by NATO countries as well as the Soviet Union, all of whom view interfering with the navigational systems of potential enemy bombers as part of a legitimate defence system although to date none has gone to the extremes the Russians may have gone to in the cases of two Korean Air Line incidents.

If it were Western policy to shoot down aerial trespassers, quite possibly there would be gunfire somewhere every month. In the US alone 'navigational errors' by LOT, the Polish airline, are commonplace, and CSA, the Czechoslovakian airline, is notorious for its 'errors' invariably over US defence areas, while Cubana, the Cuban airline, as a result of 'navigational errors' has made repeated sweeps off course over Griffiss Air Force Base in up-state New York, home of US B-52 strategic bombers.

Perhaps the modern world must consider the nightmare possibility that technology, like art, may be imitating itself, that while diplomats confer in an atmosphere of cautious hope, scientists and technicians are perfecting systems that do not require either diplomacy or hope.

Pericles only had to worry about Spartans carrying spears. For the free-world within its shrinking borders the perils and difficulties seem to be able to compound themselves. Aside from Soviet technicians experimenting on live targets with programmes for throwing navigational instruments off course and irresponsibly interfering with weather systems, there are what Lenin called 'useful idiots', people in free societies whose dedication to open exchange leads them to defy the restrictions which are essential for Western security and survival.

And other problems – Soviet agents by the thousands, encouraged by feeble laws in the West and even more feeble forms of punishment, politicians who are concerned only with how the self-serving winds blow, citizens who have no difficulty finding foreigners to peddle vital national secrets to, international trading partners who are quite often unethical at the best, deliberately dishonest at the worst, whose offices give sanctuary to industrial spies by the score, all of this possible because the free-world, after forty years, is still unable to resolve the issue of where infringement against individual rights and the responsibilities of individuals begin and end.

There is a disparity – and confusion – of thought between the captive societies and the free societies. Closed societies are not troubled with human rights, individual dignity, even the value of human life, which makes a recognition of national goals quite simple. Free societies agonize over such things as conscience, personal prerogatives, legal and constitutional checks and balances, the impropriety of government taking human life. The decision is more often than not to do nothing, or to do as little as possible. Among free people there is no clear opinion of what is a peril and what is not, or of what deserves punishment and what does not. It is this confused negativeness which makes recognition of national security goals in free societies almost impossible.

Even in blatant cases of what earlier generations called treason, convictions by law are uncommon and punishment has been a farce since the Rosenbergs were executed in the United States for passing atomic secrets to a Soviet vice-consul in 1953, an event that had unending repercussions.

In the business world, which has not traditionally suffered from an excess of ethics, entrepreneurs denounce sanctions as loudly as do the academics and scientists, on the same grounds, that they are an infringement upon freedom, but with even less justification when money rather than principles feeds their ire.

And there are plausible arguments against unilateral embargoes. They penalize some while others profit. Sweeping embargoes would not work, but they would bring unprecedented prosperity to those who feed the underground pipeline. If they worked, they would also bring very real hardship to those whose trade with what is now the Eastern bloc began as trade among neighbours a thousand years ago and whose prosperity has historically been dependent upon that trade.

But nothing is hopeless – unless it is relying upon the promises of politicians or expecting someone's irrevocable policy of disagreeable no-change to change.

For Europe, balancing upon an unpleasant economic brink, which it has periodically done, but perhaps not often as uncomfortably as at present, there is no alternative to interneighbourly trade. Britain cannot, and certainly would not, relish a return to the ethos of Stonehenge. Germany, France and Italy, while full of admiration for the Renaissance, would resist a return to that era.

Europe will trade with Europeans. Perhaps as much as three-quarters of their substance derives from that trade. America, on the other hand, as an international trader without absolute dependency on European markets, has a particular advantage. It can trade grain, cotton, fabrics, almost anything but sophisticated high technology without seriously injuring either itself or the Europeans.

If the US did not possess this advantage, plus one other, problems of a common security would be much more difficult. The other advantage is America's leadership in the field of high-tech, which the Russians have recognized to the extent that they maintain a greater network of shoppers in the US than they do in any two European countries.

Japan is also a leader in high technology but rarely as an innovator in the US sense. The clone psychology of Japan does not encourage the same degree of grassroots ingenuity encountered elsewhere. The Japanese, like the Russians, can take someone else's prototype, duplicate it and even enhance it, which they have been doing for years. Their ability to invent is less outstanding. Still, with the US technology acquired over the years, both the Japanese and the Soviets have kept pace with whatever is state-of-the-art at the moment.

The ideas come from the West. In the West the best ideas in high technology have more often than not come from the US, where the greatest high-tech drain exists. Controlling that drain brings the topic back where it began: free exchange versus control.

It is difficult to imagine how this will end. Perhaps with no control or too much control. Human nature appears to enjoy extremes. Possibly too it will end with the most ingenious people voluntarily accepting restrictions in the limited areas where they may be needed most in order to ensure Western survival, and everyone else enjoying all the irresponsible freedom they think is a birthright and which can never be taken from them.

But whatever the outcome, security for the free societies appears to rest almost exclusively on their ability to stay so far ahead, as for example with Mr Reagan's 'Star Wars' screen, that deterrent can take the place of *détente*.

Of course it would be essential that the onion dome old minds know there was such a screen, and even more essential that they be prevented from obtaining it. If the past is any measure of the future, that might be even harder than perfecting the screen.

To the present time no really significant development,

from nuclear fission to gene-splicing, to producing laser weapons, to producing intelligence-destroying mists, or missiles, or enhanced bacteriological plagues, has not been bought or stolen by Soviet agents. Some have been improved to such an extent that one small accident has killed hundreds of people. Others which were not designed to be weapons have become weapons.

If there is an ionospheric screen, and if knowledge of it is restricted to no more than a dozen top scientists and perhaps less than that number of defence department officials, there will almost certainly be one mole among them. A US officer of General Staff calibre was a Soviet mole for almost ten years.

The British have had their Philbys and Blunts and no doubt still have them. The Germans and French have had Soviet spies in their military and upper-echelon ministries. The confidant of a former West German Chancellor was a mole. A former head of Britain's Intelligence service was said by French Intelligence to have had Soviet connections. An adviser of the war-time US President Franklin Roosevelt was identified as a Soviet mole: Alger Hiss; he was convicted for passing two hundred secret state documents to an agent of an international Soviet spy ring.

Do measures exist to prevent the drain, uncover the moles, restrict the dissatisfied academics and scientists? They have always existed without being supported. If the US will not make the effort, then quite likely there will be an enduring race to stay ahead until in time the pursuers believe there is no longer a need to continue the pursuit. That time cannot be distant.

The *practice* of restriction can probably be undertaken with more hope for success than can the *politics* of restriction.

Business depends on computers. So do individuals. So do armies, navies and air forces. So do enemies who are already computerized from Leningrad to the Sea of Okhotsk. Excepting the most sophisticated computers and the constant improvements which arrive more regularly than rain, the world has been so computerized it should surprise no one if someone does not come up with a silicon implant to increase biological intelligence, replace senility and do away with retardation.

Computers, which sprang from illogical ideas, have snared the imagination as perhaps nothing else has done since the horseless carriage, electricity and the telephone. In effect, the age of electronics has been incorporated into everyday life; it belongs to everyone.

It is all well and good to arouse public concern over a possible danger, as politicians do, and perhaps place blame for past ignorance or downright duplicity where it properly belongs, but in effect recriminations and excuses serve the same illogical, and perhaps frustrating, function as teats on a man. If errors of judgement occurred as they certainly did in all the free societies or if duplicity put the free-world at risk, it is the proper work of historians to note this. For everyone else the proper concern is survival.

There will have to be restrictions.

The Computer Age is upon us. So much for that fact. It cannot be, and never could have been, maintained as a secret. A great number of people, some sincere, others not, some honest, some dishonest, some serving what they perceive as the Rights of Man, some serving Mr Reagan's 'evil empire', stand arrayed against restrictions. The sincere dissenters stand apart as believers in a lofty philosophy, as did Albert Einstein. Everyone else is at the bottom of that same hill as varied in their self-serving interests as people ordinarily are, and in the middle ground is where they will all have to meet, because whatever else they may be, excluding those who serve old minds, the inhabitants of free societies require survival.

To internationalists, as to multi-national corporations, this is no longer a world of bilateralists or isolationalism. Interdependency governs the flow of trade and capital, usually determined by market demand. It has been said that without this interchange developing countries would remain static or would regress. Certainly multi-nationals that invest in poor nations add impetus to anaemic economies, nor is it reasonable not to favour such investment. Nor are the complaints of the multi-nationals that, being intensely computerized, restrictions on overseas sales and use of computers would play havoc with their operations, without justification. Nor has this anything to do with keeping state-of-the-art electronic sophistication at home.

Computers used by the great international corporations are not advanced in most cases beyond what Eastern bloc nations already possess as a result of legal – and pipeline – acquisitions over the last fifteen years. Doubters have clear, physical evidence of this in daily newspaper displays of Soviet weaponry. For public consumption it may be well and good to pronounce for embargoes, especially if public sentiment is aroused and fearful over Russian acquisitions, but it is also irrelevant to do so. The time for restricting computer technology is past – if it were ever feasible.

In free societies computerized multi-national corporations promote trade. As part of a successful international system they provide a beneficial allocation of resources.

The electronics industry is part of this scheme. In fact, it has made it possible. By itself it has generated billions of dollars annually and has made possible the generation of billions of dollars in other industries. It performs in all advanced nations and in many that are not advanced. To restrict it would create havoc in world trade. Nor would general restrictions be successful.

At issue is the fundamental implausibility of a general embargo against ideas. Computer electronics exists and will not go away. It has spread even into the hermetic societies. As with other great ideas, when the time was opportune to change the human experience, the idea appeared which would change it.

Nevertheless, in superior state-of-the-art electronics restrictions have a definite place not in the extremes imposed from the top for reasons of political expediency nor as iron-fisted parochialism but as sensible safeguards.

As far as computers are concerned, remarkable though they undeniably are, they are an appliance, programmable refrigerators with great potential, and to whatever extent they may alter existence or serve as the 'brains' for weapons it is certain they will do both to some degree. But computers achieved notoriety as the most visible product of the electronic industry and while in fact the industry continues to produce them in increasingly sophisticated variety, actual electronic ingenuity has progressed beyond its hardware – and software – adolescence. Deprive a computer of its program and it will starve to death. A belief that computers are the ultimate wonder of the electronics age belongs in the same category of belief that considers Soviet science incapable of matching free-world innovativeness.

Computers are adjuncts of an advanced electronic technology. They are swift and efficient components of systems far advanced over anything a computer can do by itself. They are essential for their purpose. For example, in laser technology computers are a basic tool. Lasers may be able to change plant and animal forms or penetrate flesh to cure maladies, or destroy warships, aircraft and tanks, or eventually fry brains and cook the meat under helmets and inside uniforms. When used in ionospheric projects they can bring drought-induced starvation to a million Africans or they can cause unprecedentedly hot summers without rainfall in an area such as London where historically there have always been mists and moisture. A computer can do none of these things. Lasers can create three-dimensional art, a bird in flight, a field of poppies against a horizon of mountains. In comparison a computer's one-dimensional graphics are childlike. Eventually lasers may be able to change a landscape or burn a bright beacon toward distant galaxies and be seen, if anyone is watching.

If they accomplish these things, it will be through association with computers but because computers are containers of programmes they can do none of these things by themselves.

The age of high technology may have begun with computers but it did not end with them. Nor in all likelihood will it end with lasers. Somewhere down the road is a meeting between brilliance and time, the unlocking of doors which seers and mystics have dreamed of for centuries. Degenerative-free human life? Millions of acres of food-producing air? Fourth, fifth and sixth dimensions for colonization?

For as long as everything people produce is converted to weaponry, it would be unrealistic to believe humanity will not divide as it always has into those who would control the world and those who would resist such control, using weapons to accomplish both ends. Obviously there must be controls to prevent someone's super-weapon from reaching the wrong hands but because actual success is almost totally unlikely the alternative is something which will outmode the weapons, and if there is an ultimate course and both adversaries possess it, it will perhaps be called Survival.

The nation that can guarantee survival will possibly own the ultimate weapon. If it belongs to the free-world, the same adversaries of freedom who have been so active for a generation in their attempts to acquire other technology will mount a great acquisitive effort here too. No free society has not been penetrated, its secrets stolen, but in this case the thieves will acquire a technology which will destroy their prospects for domination, reduce their mountain of iron to a scrap-heap and immobilize their armies.

But survival has a horrendous price-tag.

At present there are fifty thousand nuclear warheads in the world. In the last ten years it required $33 million to eradicate smallpox; that equals five hours of the US military budget to support America's share of those warheads and maintain the US military structure.

A recent newspaper editorial noted that if, as the actuarial tables of insurance companies suggest, a human life is worth $20,000 and the alternative to survival is somewhere in the neighbourhood of 175 million Americans and 250 million Europeans dead, then, other considerations aside, the cost of survival is cheap.

But that presupposes an answer to one side of a question that has more than two sides. The ultimate statistic, the bottom line, is that basing the cost of survival on dollars, pounds, yens, roubles, Deutschmarks or whatever and using past costs as an estimate for future costs, managing to survive will bankrupt the survivors.

That is bad enough – a world without an economy – but the real tragedy is that none of this is really necessary. Those who farm the earth, heat the forges, raise the children, build the churches, the cities, the roads, the homes, create the families, the social orders, the good warm things of life, do not need any of this but such is the condition of the world that they are going to get it and pay for it because, although the entire scenario is asinine, if they mean to survive that is the only way they are going to be able to do it. The latest and most costly innovation to catch the imagination and hope of survivalists is a proposal entitled the Strategic Defence Initiative, commonly called 'Star Wars'. In a perfected operational form it could mean survival.

15
The Prelude

Although President Reagan's 1983 Strategic Defence Initiative, calling for research whose goal would be to provide a defensive shield to protect the West against Soviet nuclear missiles, touched off an international debate over what some saw as a fresh phase of the arms race, in fact it was a proposal to remedy a situation which has been worsening for years. Those who deplored taking East-West competition into space were ignoring the fact that space has played a major part in international relations for more than twenty years, with an increasing degree of importance each year since 1967.

The Strategic Defence Initiative was the predictable result of on-going space relevance and was new only to the extent that it proposed concentrating scatter-shot technologies toward one goal rather than allowing them to continue as unco-ordinated efforts.

Fifty thousand nuclear missiles amounted to a ridiculous redundancy. A third that number were enough to destroy civilization, and the accumulation was continuing along with increasingly sophisticated and expensive systems of delivery, proliferating Intelligence offensives and hypocritical limitation discussions. The Strategic Defence Initiative (SDI) suggested a fresh approach to an old problem: how to protect the free-world and, providing the other side were interested, how to achieve a defence against what it saw as a threat from the West.

Until the advent of the Strategic Defence Initiative (SDI) idea, free-world defence policies reflected the fragmented confusion of sixteen NATO countries.

In the face of Soviet nuclear deployment threatening Europe, and the US response which included placing

American missiles in Europe as a counterforce, Europeans ran hot and cold. Some objected to US missiles in their countries, preferring to be defenceless. Others favoured the missiles. Both the illusionists and the pragmatists had legitimate convictions, pragmatists for favouring rational defence and illusionists for believing the situation was asinine. The SDI concept proposed neutralizing nuclear warheads, something likely to find favour with both sides and everyone else who dreads the alternative regardless of their ideologies or their politics. Its basic thrust was toward a co-ordinated effort through advanced technology which would neutralize everyone's stockpile of nuclear weapons.

However, such has been the frantic pace of technological progress that, while strident disarray was loudest on the ground, the adversarial confrontation had been moving into space for years, as high as 22,000 miles above the Earth, and when this was publicized the disarray, and fear, increased, abetted by Soviet dismay based upon a genuine concern that, regardless of how competent their R&D and S&T have become and regardless of how heavily involved they are in the exploitation of space, they cannot economically keep this up indefinitely. They had another cause for anxiety: if SDI achieved practical results and nullified their enormous accumulation of nuclear armament, it could become subject to a strategic melt-down. That could include the military exploitation of space which they have been extravagantly funding since 1969, an outgrowth of the Soviet fascination with extra-terrestrial weaponry.

Worldwide that fascination was anything but new. Scientific puttering had been cluttering space with experimental trash for years. Defence organizations had been lofting sky-spies euphemistically called 'weather satellites' for at least two decades. As early as 1967, after suitable deliberation within the United Nations organization, a treaty was drafted to bind its signatories not to put weapons into Earth orbit. It was a fumbling first effort. Subsequent treaties had the advantage of more expertise but the 1967 treaty demonstrated that there was a dawning anxiety. It was to be the forerunner of a ream of treaties, and its innocence was displayed through use of the word 'orbit' meaning to circumnavigate, to travel completely around something. Intercontinental Ballistic Missiles (ICBMs) do not 'go around'; they rise, achieve a curving trajectory and fall on a target. They go only one way.

The treaty also said space was to be used for 'peaceful purposes'. 'Peaceful' meant non-aggressive. Satellites were not aggressive. They were not armed. But they spied and were built to eavesdrop, to record military and other conversations and to provide early warning. If satellites were exempt from treaty restrictions, presumably so were ASAT vehicles, anti-satellite satellites. They did not have to be armed; they simply had to be aimed to collide with other satellites at high speed.

So the race was on. Two years after the UN treaty was signed, the Soviet Union established an anti-satellite programme, the PKO. In 1970 it tested an anti-satellite prototype which could reach a target in space (low orbit) and explode alongside it, so there was a weapon in space three years after the 1967 UN treaty, thirteen years before the Reagan SDI proposal. During the sixteen-year period satellites proliferated, and approximately three-quarters of all satellites ever launched have been for military purposes. They have become vital for monitoring the stockpile for mass destruction on Earth.

Exploitation of space for other than peaceful purposes began when the first surveillance satellite was launched and has continued ever since. Surveillance satellites are extensions of military systems. As weapons they are in the same category as bomb-sights, periscopes and the eyes of soldiers and have become every bit as vital as those other things are. They are indispensable to defence, and opponents consider them offensive weapons. In the past they were physically harmless but presently some are suitable for lethal enhancement and can become deadly weapons.

They have also become the basis for changing national policies.

For twenty years the US and USSR lived with a balance of terror based on the premise that there was no real defence against an attack by nuclear missiles of which both sides had enough to devastate the other. This was called the Mutual Assured Destruction (MAD) strategy, and surveillance satellites verified for both sides that each had enough missiles to destroy the other. They also photographed missile fields, and that encouraged strategists on both sides to think in terms of destroying one another's weapons instead of populations, which was the MAD philosophy. This led to the current counterforce philosophy, made possible through satellite surveillance as well as improved aiming systems.

An Intelligence estimate of the number of satellites presently in operation is 450 but an actual count is not possible, not entirely because neither the US nor the USSR is free with numbers but also because other nations have launched them, as have a number of civilian Intelligence, scientific and private-sector organizations.

Nevertheless, in relation to what matters, conflict or the avoidance of it between the superpowers, the 450 approximation must be reasonably close, bearing in mind that it cannot be accurate because both the US and the USSR are heavily engaged in programmes to lift more and improved satellites and that in the neighbourhood of 120 additional military satellites are launched annually.

Satellites are not permanent fixtures, although if they can reach space undamaged and deploy themselves higher than a few hundred kilometres, where there is essentially no air, even though they may be too delicate to survive in the atmosphere or under the force of Earth's gravity where they could collapse under their own weight, they can survive a relatively long time. They are vulnerable to meteorites and the kinds of space trash irresponsible humanity has left up there. They are also vulnerable to extreme temperature changes and charged particles caught in Earth's magnetic field plus damaging levels of electrical forces. If attacked, most would be vulnerable to anything which would 'blind' their vision-sensors. Generally, to the present time satellites have not been built to withstand attack, nor has the loss of satellites from whatever cause been considered critical because replacements are available and satellites are relatively inexpensive.

Since the Soviet Union lofted an experimental satellite

about twenty-five years ago and the first 'killer satellite' since then, space has been aggressively exploited notwithstanding interminable 'talks' in Geneva and elsewhere. Regardless of non-proliferations accords, the 'Space Wars' concept is here to stay. The reliance on space vehicles by both superpowers has made this as indisputable as it has made satellites indispensable. Eighty per cent of US military communications are transmitted by satellite; in many instances they provide the only link between Washington and its air, sea and land commanders, and the same is true of the Soviet Union.

About half of all newly launched satellites are surveillance vehicles. Most function in low orbits, about 150 to 400 kilometres (93–249 miles) above Earth. They collect high-resolution images which can be recorded on film and jettisoned for recovery by ground crews or projected by electronic transmission, passed through other satellites to receiving stations on the ground. These satellites are especially vulnerable to 'blinding'.

'Ferret' satellites monitor radio spectrums to pick up signals transmitted in foreign countries, and some have the ability to 'hear' conversations being conveyed on Earth by simple hand-held transmitters. They also detect and record signals from missile ranges, military traffic, sea lanes and aerial corridors. US ferrets have routinely monitored transmissions from the Russian missile facilities on the Kamchatka Peninsula.

Early warning satellites can detect heat changes and tailrace emissions of ICBMs being launched, track the course of aircraft by exhaust heat and give almost immediate notice of possible nuclear attacks with sufficient time to allow for retailiation.

The latest photo-reconnaissance satellites at high level can provide perfect resolution of objects on Earth no larger than a hat and can distinguish between civilian and military attire. They can also distinguish between camouflage shrubbery and live plants and penetrate clouds and drakness, as well as monitor in detail work in progress in shipyards, missile-silo fields and farms.

Weather and navigational satellites can guide ships, aircraft and land vehicles, predict storms as well as periods of clear weather and direct missiles to targets. Eighteen satellites of the US Navstar Global Positioning System can pinpoint locations anywhere in the world, resulting in ships, aircraft or artillery being precisely on course. They can also ensure accuracy for bomber pilots in the worst weather and allow cruise missiles to make corrections while on course toward targets.

In relation to what preceded them, modern satellites are an epitome of sophisticated technology. According to the way they are put into orbit, meaning angle in relation to speed and height, their course can be shaped for maximum efficiency. Gone are the days of educated guesswork.

Soviet reconnaissance satellites are put into low orbit to reach the lowest point of their perigee over areas of special interest. Early warning, communication and navigational satellites are more nearly stationary in order to operate at maximum efficiency above points on Earth they are designed to monitor. They accomplish this by being placed in geo-stationary orbits at an altitude above the equator at a velocity to match the Earth's rotation.

It was an increasing dependency of US armed forces on these fragile space assets that prompted development of the space shuttle. It can take satellites to space, launch and care for them. US space shuttles can carry close to 30,000 kilograms (66,150 pounds) and put it into a 180 kilometre (112 miles) orbit. Presently the USSR is building a larger shuttle with a 60,000-kilo (132,300 pounds) load capacity that can put 150,000 kilos (330,750) pounds into low orbit.

As the importance and proliferation of satellites have escalated, so has the need to neutralize them. This is the initial phase of the 'Star Wars' concept, the prelude.

Three years after the Soviet Union developed its first satellite killer the US tested a Western version. In 1984 an improved prototype killer rocket armed with a dummy warhead was successfully launched. Eleven months later an operational version was tested above Vandenberg Air Force Base in California. It was launched from mounts under the belly of an F-15's jetfighter at the approximate apex of the F-15's climb, about ten miles. The rocket's warhead, which was about the size of a beer bottle, had an infra-red guidance system and was aimed at a distant star because the US Congress voted against a live trial.

The idea behind the development of this projectile was that infra-red emissions from a satellite would serve as a homing device, like a magnet. The warhead did not require an explosive charge. Destruction resulted from a collision at high speed. Basically this was a duplication of the Soviet staellite killer but with an improved launching ability, and the US version was not armed and did not detonate. Presently the proposal is to have at least two F-15 squadrons available for deployment by the late 1980s to launch these rockets.

What makes such a weapon feasible is the relatively slow speed of satellites, the fact that most are fragile and are in low orbit. The rocket is a defensive vehicle; it cannot injure people. Concurrent with the ASAT programme which developed this rocket, the US undertook deployment of a missile-silo system of protection against ICBM fields which was also entirely defensive.

If Soviet strategists doubted that the US retaliatory missile force could be destroyed on the ground by a pre-emptive attack, they might be deterred from launching one. It is this doubt on both sides that is the basis for deterrence.

The technology to provide such defence is at hand and could be operational within three years. Simultaneously, completion of a counterforce capability, which would enable the US to destroy Soviet ICBMs shortly after launch and before they could get near US targets which would add to deterrence, is also in process of development. Success for this project and others is dependent upon the efficiency of operating satellites. It makes them of critical importance to military strategy, and that means they must be treated as part of an enemy's arsenal. In consequence of the need to neutralize them, a number of anti-satellite projects have been developed.

In June 1982 the Soviet Union launched a killer satellite from its Tyuratam cosmodrome in central Asia, manoeuvred it by ground control into the orbit of a target spacecraft 965.4 kilometres (600 miles) above earth and destroyed the target. This was a stationary, unsophisticated system. In comparsion the US killer satellite, which is less than six metres (twenty feet) long and carried aloft beneath an F-15, can be launched from any accessible airfield in the world, and where it requires about eight hours for the Soviet vehicle to reach a target, because the US version is launched from sixteen kilometres (ten miles) into space it requires much less time to reach its target.

Neither the US nor the USSR at present has killer satellites capable of reaching the most critical early warning and communication satellites which rotate with the Earth's orbit at 32,180 kilometres (20,000) in space. But that will certainly change as the necessity of neutralizing sky-eyes increases.

Of present concern to US authorities are four primary and several secondary Soviet satellites. The four are the RORSAT, or radar ocean reconnaissance satellite; the ELINT-3, an Intelligence satellite that employs a record-and-playback mode that can pick up anything that emits a radio signal; the EORSAT, which in conjunction with RORSAT vehicles tracks warships but can also detect radar sites, operating airfields as well as airborne guidance and control systems; and finally ELINT-4 satellite, to be put aloft in late 1985, a more advanced Intelligence asset than its predecessor, ELINT-3.

Secondary satellites include the Soviet series of military space stations, the 'Salyuts'. Altogether the total number of Soviet satellites of concern to the US is about forty and includes NAVSAT types used to guide Soviet ballistic missile submarines. Neutralizing these satellites would seriously impair undersea navigation.

On the other side, of concern to the Russians is the Lockheed 'Big Bird' satellite equipped with high-resolution cameras which passes over every area on Earth twice each twenty-four hours. 'Big Birds' have a 'life' of about two hundred days. In consequence one is launched every six months.

Another is the CIA KH 11 surveillance satellite. The KH 11 programme has been in operation since 1976 and is exclusively for Intelligence-gathering. KH 11s have a life-expectancy of about one year and orbit higher than more conventional surveillance vehicles.

The NATO-3, which has a life-expectancy of about three years, is of particular concern to the Soviets because it is used to provide communication between Europe and the US, and the US MILSTAR system which is another communication satellite, in this case designed to provide contact under combat conditions. Because it has been anticipated that the Soviets would concentrate on eliminating MILSTAR assets first, they have been built to withstand both physical and electronic attack.

Two additional US satellites which would certainly be targeted for early destruction by the Soviets in the event of war are the SKYNET, used by the United Kingdom in geo-stationary orbit above the Seychelles to provide immediate capability for ground contacts between distance areas, and the SDS-7, a communication satellite for bombers in polar regions, those capable of reaching the Kamchatka Peninsula by way of Alaska or of attacking Russia over the North Pole.

All surveillance, communication and navigational satellites would be targets, and while orders of priority may exist with the Soviets as they do with the Americans, the actual response time to shift from Priority One to Priority Two targets would be only a matter of moments. And certainly the need to neutralize space assets will increase as their numbers and sophistication increase. Examples would be the LEASAT geo-stationary worldwide communication system, a great improvement over single-system vehicles, which consists of four vehicles; TRW company's FLSATCOM, a US Navy communication system consisting of five vehicles with a sixth in reserve; and TRW's Phase II Air Force communication system which consists of sixteen satellites and is shared with the United Kingdom's defence forces.

A later version, the Phase III launched in 1982, reflected the view of a time of particular East-West antagonism that such systems should be protected. It was 'hardened' against attack. 'Hardening' cannot provide immunity, it can only protect satellites against some forms of attack, but as satellites assume wider roles in national defence it can be assumed that considerable effort will be expended to improve this condition.

To a great extent satellites have assumed the function of earlier Distant Early Warning (DEW) radar systems. Their ability to 'see' above and beyond horizons as well as to communicate with words and pictures instead of 'blips' and 'bleeps' is an advantage. Also, the technique of hugging the ground to escape radar detection as cruise missiles have done is less likely to succeed with satellites. Further, satellites provide a better service than surveillance aircraft. They could have prevented embarrassment for America during the Eisenhower Administration when a US spy-plane, the U2, was shot down over Russia. The U2 was within range of ground-fire, something satellites are not. Nor are satellites dependent upon fuel tanks. The best spy aircraft have a short time in the air.

Satellites are limited only by their 'life-span', which in lower ranges can be as short as a few weeks and in higher ranges can be as long as several years.

Spy-planes can monitor limited areas. Satellites routinely monitor the world and do it as often as several times a day.

Pilots of surveillance aircraft are vulnerable because spy-planes are usually unarmed. Shooting down a pilot could cause, and has caused, some ugly situations. Downing a spy satellite, even if it were not done surreptitiously, leaving no trace and despite statements to the contrary, is unlikely to cause a serious confrontation. Both sides have many replacements, no life has been lost, and although it has been said that downing a US satellite would be considered as an 'act of war', probably because no one would want to look ridiculous, beyond sending someone a stiff note of protest the matter would end there.

The widening scope of the satellite's function, as well as the dependency armed nations have come to place on it, makes it almost certain that there will be 'incidents'. The US has bases as distant from North America as Turkey and Africa. The USSR has bases in Cuba and Nicaragua. There is no faster way for distant outposts to communicate with home than by satellite.

In periods of peace, tampering will certainly occur. In other times Intelligence, communication and navigational satellites will be among the first casualties.

The problem of destroying satellite effectiveness either through 'blinding' or by disturbing navigational systems is different from knocking them out of the sky, a clearly hostile act.

Low-level satellites are vulnerable to currently available anti-satellite technology but the assets in high orbit, up to 22,000 miles in space, are in a different category, although according to some authorities and the US Joint Chiefs of Staff they could be vulnerable to electronic-pulse effects from explosions above the atmosphere or other electronic countermeasures. R&D in this field is underway in the US and Intelligence satellites using high-resolution cameras have provided evidence that Soviet scientists and engineers are currently working on directed-energy programmes whose purpose would be to neutralize high-orbiting satellites.

The US General Accounting Office which commonly disparages Department of Defence proposals has said that alternative technologies for neutralizing Russian satellites should include investigation of three kinds of anti-satellite lasers, ground-based, space-based and airborne – as with the F-15 project which the General Accounting Office did not like because of what it considered excessive cost in relation to possible accomplishment.

The search for anti-satellite systems has been part of the Department of Defence's acquisition policy for a long time, and lasers are at the top of the list because satellites are very susceptible to them.

Lasers are part of President Reagan's Strategic Defence Initiative – 'Star Wars' – project. They too present problems areas but at least, as weapons against Soviet satellites and what else may come over the horizon later, they offer greater potential than other ideas.

Directed-energy particle beams, for example, weaken through diffusion the farther they travel, which they have in common with other forms of directed energy. There is evidently a way to cause their propagation in space but the technology to accomplish this does not appear to be close at hand. Another proposal, microwaves, also become widening spectrums as they travel, which means that in a distant environment inhabited by hundreds of satellites many of which would be 'friendly' microwaves would probably damage more than just hostile satellites.

But laser technology, which has been spectacular in some areas such as photography and health care, has not been as spectacular in other areas. Sophistication is certainly possible but there are major problems to inhibit miraculous breakthroughs.

For all directed energy systems envisioned as weapons against satellites, the difficulties of distance are perhaps the least of the problems, but with lasers there is an established R&D base to work from. Scientists have been experimenting with lasers for a number of years. It has been established what a laser can do as a concentrated beam: burn through steel, for example. But this has been accomplished from short distances, initially about one metre (three feet).

At present a laser beam aimed at a low-orbit satellite at an altitude of 360 kilometres – 220 miles – above Earth, could cause trouble for the satellite if the beam could be prevented from diffusing. At 36,000 kilometres (22,000 miles) a ground-aimed laser would become 100 metres (300 feet) in diameter and lack force. The difference between laser intensity at higher orbit and lower would be about one ten-thousandth unless a large reflector were used, meaning its effectiveness in high orbit would be dissipated.

At lower orbit, where guidance, weather, Intelligence, communication and navigational satellites operate and where a controlled beam would have its best potential, success could occur. Satellites which depend upon optical or infra-red sensors or 'eyes' could be blinded. Normally their 'sight' comes from silicon detectors, although some use infra-red wavelengths. The infra-red varieties are more vulnerable than the silicon variety but both are susceptible to disruption by brilliance and heat. They can be 'blinded' by illumination greater than their sensors are designed to accept, perhaps not permanently but for long enough periods of time to prevent observation of areas on the ground they are supposed to be monitoring. Permanent damage is possible in a peripheral sense. If 'blinding' causes overloading of electrical circuits, the entire system can be permanently damaged.

The satellite can also be made inoperable through thermal injury – heating to temperatures that would destroy the material of which a satellite is made, for example, or by physically damaging a lens, possibly shattering it by intense heat.

Disorientation is also possible. Satellites are oriented on something, aligned to take their bearings from the Earth, stars or sun. This is how their antennae are kept pointing in the correct direction. They do this with sensors which can be disoriented by laser beams.

The solar cells which generate power for many satellites, although designed to handle considerable amounts of light such as comes from the sun, are vulnerable to heavy doses of great brilliance of the kind lasers can generate and transmit.

Satellites have another weakness. Being subject to unfiltered sunlight in space which is considerably greater than filtered sunlight at Earth-level, they dissipate it through radiation. But radiative cooling is slower than convective cooling; satellites cannot get rid of the kind of intense, sustained heat a laser beam can project fast enough to prevent heat damage to both the vehicle and its circuitry.

However, countermeasure 'hardening' of satellites with coatings which would evaporate under laser attack to hasten cooling, or which would deflect heat, are being tested.

The General Accounting Office's recommendation that different kinds of lasers can be considered came in the wake of this 'hardening' and other research already in progress. Those recommendations emphasized the direction the US 'Star Wars' project was already taking, testing lasers and other non-nuclear methods of neutralizing the Soviet arsenal of sky-weapons and suggesting – to the hopeful – that as this kind of technology progresses it may mark a developing continuum which would do more than just neutralize satellites. It might even neutralize nuclear missiles as well; they too could be susceptible to directed energy disorientation. They too operate by sensors and electrical circuitry.

Or this may amount to a yearning for Hyperborea. The Soviet Union has inaugurated a crash-programme to improve its space technology which includes an intensified Intelligence-acquisition effort.

In quality and sophistication there is a gap between East and West but in developing capabilities to overcome this gap there is no gap. Their problem will not depend on the ability to achieve parity in space technology: it will depend upon economics.

16

The Toymakers

Twenty years ago an article in the classified Red Army publication *Military Thought* said that, 'The mastering of space [is] a prerequisite for achieving victory in war.'

At that time and for approximately the ensuing two decades the Soviet economy was increasingly dedicated to that and related military objectives. With an annual GNP heading toward $2 trillion, military expansion and improvement were possible. Beyond that period undermining the economy through expenditures that drained it, rather than enhanced it through capital growth, caused stagnation.

Soviet officials charged with responsibility for economic improvement have not been as noted for their ability to perform effectively in areas of their official concern as they have been for their willingness to support the military drain.

By 1985, at the expense of the capital sector, the military was pre-eminent. What is specifically unclear at present, although evident as a factor, is how much longer this can continue.

Certainly this problem is a reason for USSR efforts to discredit the Strategic Defence Initiative. Whether discrediting is effective or not has little bearing on what has been accomplished to the present in the Soviet drive to assure the dual military objectives of global support for its armed forces and denying the use of space to the US in the event of war, and it appears that nothing better exemplifies the differences in superpower philosophies than this offensive Soviet aggressiveness and the SDI strategy of defence.

US policy has become a strategy of seeking means for neutralizing what probably cannot be physically overcome – the enormous accumulation of Soviet weaponry.

USSR policy is committed to intimidation by projecting a national prestige of overpowering military influence; an evident willingness to wage war.

What worries sceptics of the Strategic Defence Initiative is whether it remains true that defence is inferior to offence, when more is at stake than a football game and when being wrong can be cataclysmic.

What, then, has the Soviet Union accomplished during that twenty-year period of capital drain other than an overwhelming military presence on Earth and a horde of military-serving satellites aloft? Whether or not it can continue as a participant in the arms race, what has it achieved that would compel the West to continue the competition?

For one thing the Soviets have perfected an operational space-station system, the 'Salyut' series. Throughout most of 1984 their Salyut 7 vehicle manned by a crew of three conducted military experiments, one of which was aimed at nullifying Western reliance on submarines carrying nuclear missiles capable of threatening the USSR and said by Western authorities to be of particular value because submerged submarines are not visually detectable.

Soviet experiments from low orbit using lasers and satellites had as their objective detecting subtle changes on ocean surfaces for locating submarines. They were also interested in the feasibility of the USSR's three hundred nuclear-armed aircraft penetrating US borders over the North Pole.

They could have achieved gratifying results here. Ground-hugging cruise missiles can be fired as far as 2,896 kilometres (1,800 miles) from their targets by Soviet aeroplanes and penetrate wide gaps in the North American early warning radar screen. A Canadian committee has reported that, 'At present hostile bombers could fly undetected into the heart of North America and attack US deterrent forces ...' without being detected by radar. Supporting this view a US Air Force General, Bruce Brown, has stated that, 'At low altitudes there are miles of coastline where bombers (and presumably cruise missiles) can penetrate our airspace without detection.'

Could this be accomplished despite the monitoring of US watch-dog satellite systems?

According to Intelligence sources Soviet cosmonauts have successfully experimented with satellite-blinding techniques for short periods at low orbit. Louis Marquet, director of DOD's Strategic Defence Initiative organization's directed-energy research, said in early 1984 that if the Soviets '... marshalled their technology, they could, in principle, blind any of our satellites today'.

In the ensuing fifteen months, up to May 1985, it became fairly clear that earlier experiments at the Sary Shagan proving-ground in the southern USSR were successful; the Soviets could blind US satellites.

Additional examples of the Soviet aggressiveness which forces the US to compete include broadening the base of the Russian drive to dominate space. Since 1983 they have been perfecting a space vehicle to dwarf the Salyut. It will weigh 101.6 tonnes (100 tons) and accommodate a crew of twelve. Its primary purpose will be to study practical methods for deploying large space-based weapons including those which can blind or destroy US satellites. This vehicle, third of a heavyweight class, can carry a 150,000 kilogram (330,750 pounds) payload to an altitude of 180 kilometres (112 miles). In comparision the US shuttles carry a payload of 95,000 kilos (209,475 pounds) to 180 kilometres (112 miles). At least one of the Soviet's Space Transportation Systems (STSs) is probably a result of pipeline acquisition; it is very nearly a duplication of the US space shuttle. The noticeable difference is that on the Soviet STS the main engines are not on the orbiter.

At the Tyuratam proving-ground launch and support facilities are presently prepared to test new STSs. Advanced prototypes use the STS's own core rockets in one series. In another series a new medium-lift launch system has apparently been designed for fast sequences of launches. And there is a small STS resembling a delta-winged military aircraft which has been fired into low orbit at least three times from the Kasputin Yar facility near the Caspian Sea and which may be compatible with the low-orbit rapid-launch medium-lift system. There is also a unique ferrying support vehicle to be used in space to move supplies and equipment from one space station to another.

All of these systems are for military objectives or in support of them. Obviously the Soviet Union has no intention of limiting the exploitation of space for defensive purposes. Current systems are part of a policy to launch at least a hundred vehicles a year, to increase Soviet R&D toward achieving two ends: military domination of space, and preeminence in space technology by increasing the weight-load capacity of Soviet space vehicles.

At present Soviet scientists and engineers are developing a heavy-lift station estimated to weigh many times more than their largest booster can loft at the present time, with a payload capacity in excess of anything Western authorities see as practical given the status of present technology. They conduct a minimum of four times as many heavy launches annually as the US does. The most advanced of their manned space vehicles present opportunities for planetary exploration, and since seventy per cent of Soviet space vehicles are military systems, in the view of scientists their objective may be the establishment of Soviet bases on planetary bodies. But all this must be in the long view. More relevant is domination at much lower elevations, and on Earth.

Toward that goal their nearly operational SKYLAB system, designed to accommodate up to twelve crewmen, to be followed by much larger system to be manned by a hundred crewmen, would move any conflict between the superpowers into an area where large armies would probably not be feasible and where technicians of company size would have the ability to decide the outcome of hostilities.

It may well be that the cost of all this, which has already created difficulties, may shortly be responsible for a national crisis. Nevertheless, the level of effort has not slackened during the 1980s and a projected growth for the Soviet space effort is expected to surpass overall military spending until approximately the year 2000, the objective being to achieve superiority and to integrate Soviet space systems with conventional armed forces on Earth.

There is no indication of a slackening. The alternative for the US is to match Soviet aggressiveness with up-graded systems of defence. Over the previous twenty years Soviet cultivation of sophisticated space technologies, concurrent with growth in the conventional R&D sector in order to achieve maximum co-ordination between both, has resulted in expansion of two large, active nuclear test facilities, one at Semipalitinsk, the other at Novaya Zemlya.

Neither superpower at present is capable of sustaining a war against Earth, but both have developed systems which would permit *direction* of such a war from space. Their main objective thus far has been oriented toward attacking each other in space and to direct ground-launched missiles as well as to provide space-based defence against hostile missiles and give warning of their approach.

With the advent of ultimate sophistication this will change. When laser and particle-beam technology becomes practical, along with other nasty little surprises presently in less advanced stages of research and development, attacks against Earth from space may be possible. Earth armies could become anachronistic, war-fighting could move to space, and the diffusion of non-nuclear directed-energy weapons, which at present make concentrations of light emissions relatively harmless if they must travel far, may be overcome to the extent that lethal concentrations will provide a means for frying human beings block by block, square by square, hour by hour, simply by making slow sweeps from space.

Co-ordination between Soviet space stations and ground forces including areas of both which have lacked finesse in the past may be relied upon to possess it in the future, but even if it were not achieved, an inescapable relevancy here is that while Soviet tanks for example may not be as sophisticated as US tanks, which employ on-board electronic guidance and aiming systems, fifty thousand Soviet tanks can roll over thirteen thousand elite tanks. In space the first Soviet space stations to achieve orbit with or without comparable sophistication will be in a shoot-down position above any foreign stations approaching from below.

This axiom carries over to nuclear missiles. Both sides possess satellite ability for early warning and guidance for megatonnage assault with Soviet capability increasing at a faster rate.

While the necessity for keeping abreast is obvious, the West still spends less and therefore does not produce as varied an assortment of advanced Intercontinental Ballistic Missiles (ICBMs) as do the Russians; sophistication which at one time belonged to the Americans in many cases no longer does.

The USSR has 8,240 verifiable nuclear warheads. Of that total 5,800 are on land-based missiles. In contrast the US has 11,900 nuclear warheads with fewer than twenty per cent on land-based missiles, the rest divided between submarine and aerial delivery systems.

Up to 1984 Soviet silo-launchers numbered 1,398. Of those 818 have been up-moded since 1972 with roughly half having been modernized to present standards over the past five years. All 818 have been 'hardened' against attack. One hundred and fifty sites are for sustaining SS-17s (Model 3), while 308 are for SS-18s (Model 4) and 306 launchers are for SS-19s (Model 3). Along with recent additions ranging from SS-20s upwards, these are the world's most sophisticated ICBMs.

Deployment of operational Soviet ICBMs in all categories, land, sea and air, translatable into terms that hurt, equals 6,500 redundant warheads – an enormous over-kill ratio.

The US deployed 1,033 missiles, roughly the same number as Russian land-based ICBMs but until about 1980 with fewer warheads – 7,280. Since 1980 additional warheads have given the US a lead and with the new MX 'Peacekeeper' missile each of which is to have ten warheads to counteract an accelerated Soviet programme, equality will remain close because current plans call for the manufacture and deployment of about seventy MXs.

From SS-18s upwards Soviet missiles are likely to be more accurate than US ICBMs and carry more Multiple Independently Targeted Re-entry Vehicles (MIRVs) – warheads – than the most modern current US ICBM the Minuteman III*.

Model 4 Soviet SS-18s carry ten MIRVs. Model 3 SS-19s

---

* The Russians acquired specifications of the Minuteman missile from an American. See page 58.

carry six. The US Minuteman III carries three, and the Soviet Model 4 SS-18 was designed to destroy 'hardened' ICBM missile silos which house Minutemen IIIs in the US with each of the SS-18's ten warheads carrying twenty times the destructive power of nuclear devices developed during World War II. As currently deployed, Soviet Model 4 SS-18s could destroy ninety per cent of US missile silos using two nuclear MIRVs against each silo. The Model 3 SS-19 has the same capability and can also be targeted against Europe and Asia.

Scaling downwards from SS-18s and SS-17s to SS-11s which were developed in 1966, range and destructive capability diminishes, but with 580 of these older ICBMs in silos ready to be launched, the danger does not really diminish very much.

Insofar as it has been possible, a consistent part of Soviet strategic policy not to replace older ICBMs but to bring them up to current standards contrasts significantly with US policy of dismantling older models.

Soviet development of ICBMs with as many as ten MIRVs beginning with the SS-18s, SS-19s and SS-20 models gives the USSR a possible slight lead over the Americans, who did not concentrate on extensive MIRVing until later. It was never the number of missiles that mattered: it was the number of warheads.

All silo-based ICBMs are stationary and therefore targetable, and even though Soviet SS-17, SS-18 and SS-19 missiles are housed in the world's most 'hardened' silos, they are vulnerable.

The older Soviet SS-16, a solid-fuel, three-stage ICBM with a single warhead, was capable of becoming mobile. Along with other current ICBMs being tested in the Soviet far north, at the Plestsk proving-ground, this probably reflected a change in Soviet strategy, perhaps the outgrowth of refinement in ICBMs which favours mobility. It certainly minimizes vulnerability.

It also makes counting warheads more difficult. Silos are unmistakably silos. Their characteristics remain evident even through camouflage. Their location and numbers can be verified by satellite surveillance.

Mobile Soviet ICBMs began in experimental stages as early as the 1960s, some on wheeled conveyor systems, some on railroad tracks, some on tank-like track-laying systems, more recently in submarines and as airborne components of aircraft. Satellite surveillance has been able to verify some of these mobile ICBM systems but where it may matter most, in the air or under the sea, verification is not possible beyond assuming that a certain class of submarine or aircraft was designed to carry warheads. From this point forward, nose-counting enters the realm of 'best estimate', not a very reassuring basis for survival.

Soviet submarines provide a fair example. The USSR has the world's largest ballistic missile submarine fleet for strategic attack. By January 1985 there were sixty-four Soviet submarines rigged to carry 981 nuclear-tipped missiles. This does not include fifteen older ships carrying forty-five missiles whose range does not allow them to travel far. Nor does it include two Soviet submarines excluded from the sixty-two SSBN (nuclear submarine) limit established by the Strategic Arms Limitations Talk (SALT) I.

Sixteen Soviet submarines built within the last seven years carry 264 MIRV-warhead ballistic missiles, and two-thirds of the Soviet Union's submarines capable of launching MIRVed missiles are in the long-range category. They routinely patrol the seas off Europe and the US. These ships are also capable of firing ballistic missiles at targets in the US and Europe without leaving Soviet waters.

Ballistic-missile submarines are recognizable as such. The guesswork involves how many warheads are aboard. The most modern Soviet submarines are of the Typhoon class. These are the largest submarines in the world. They displace 25,000 tons, one-third more than US Trident-class vessels. Typhoons carry SS-N-20 solid-propellant MIRVed SLBMs (Submarine Launched Ballistic Missiles). They can operate in any sea including beneath the Arctic ice ledge. Their range permits travel to any area, and because the range of their ICBMs is 8,300 kilometres (5,158 miles), there is no target on Earth they cannot reach. By the 1990s the USSR could have as many as eight Typhoon-class submarines in operation.

Typhoons are recognizable as ballistic-missile submarines.

Intelligence assumptions are based on what they can carry. It is assumed they would not put to sea with less than full capacity.

Soviet Delta-class submarines are also SLBM vessels. Their missiles have been SS-N-18s but recently the Soviets have been experimenting with a new, large, long-range liquid-propelled SLBM designed as the SS-N-23. It will carry more warheads and have greater throw-weight. It will also be more accurate than SS-N-18s and it may be put aboard the Delta-class ships.

Delta III SSBNs are also recognizable as ballistic-missile submarines. So are the Yankee-class older vessels. Intelligence estimates based upon the number of Soviet submarines known to be SLBM-capable provide a clue as to the Russian ability for delivering nuclear missiles, and the type of missile these ships carry suggests the number of warheads.

Estimates are probably adequate any time there is an over-kill capability.

The Soviet Union has three classes of Nuclear Ballistic Missile submarines: the Hotel, Yankee, Delta and Typhoon. The most advanced Hotel-class ship has six launching tubes for SS-N-18 missiles. The best Yankee-class ship has twelve tubes for the launching of SS-N-17 missiles. The best Delta-class submarine has twenty tubes and carries SS-N-20 ballistic missiles.

As opposed to counting missiles to determine destructive capability, in which case missiles count for less than the number of warheads they carry, with submarines as delivery systems while warheads remain critical, the delivery systems are equally so, particularly if the SLBMs they carry do not possess great range. In this case the Soviet nuclear-missile fleet of sixty-four ships outnumbers the US nuclear-missile fleet. In 1967 the US had forty-one SSBNs, each rigged to carry sixteen missiles (Polaris type). Presently the US SSBN fleet consists of thirty-two ships. The total number of missiles carried is 568 which can deliver 5,152 MIRV warheads.* The total number of nuclear missiles carried by

---

* 5,152 MIRVed warheads deliver 333 megatons. One megaton equals one million tons of TNT.

Soviet SSBNs at a lower-range estimate would be approximately 3,200. The number of MIRVed warheads could be as low as that number of many times higher.

There is a third leg of this war-fighting triad: aircraft which would serve as delivery systems for nuclear weapons. It has been said they would be less vulnerable than silo-based ICBMs but that is debatable. They certainly could not be as 'hardened' against ground-to-air missiles and in comparison with submerged submarines, another leg of the triad, their vulnerability would be overwhelming. Up to the present time locating submerged submarines has not been very satisfactory. Locating aircraft even of the supersonic kind has been more than a military pastime for fifty years. With the development of radar and more recently infra-red-equipped satellites, even night-flying aeroplanes can be located.

Surveillance aircraft flying too high to be seen or heard had a brief period of popularity before succumbing to sophisticated satellites that could locate them and track them. At best they served a gap between World War II and the satellite era. At worst their limitations made them vulnerable to a fuel-storage capacity which strictly limited their versatility.

At the speed with which war-making technologies have pressed ahead, the Soviet Union's two to three hundred bombers and the 325 owned by the Americans, along with hundreds of additional support and protection aircraft, may shortly to some extent share the prospects of Poland's cavalry, the largest horse-soldier organization in the world when Germany attacked at dawn on 1 September 1939 using a spearhead of *Panzergruppen*.

In the era of detection-satellites aloft and deadly ground-to-air missiles from below, even with an ability to 'blind' the satellites, bombers are at very high risk. Modernizing them for launching cruise as well as air-to-ground, air-to-air and even satellite-killing missiles still leaves them as exposed to detection and destruction as they always have been except that at present there are greatly improved methods for downing them.

NATO maintains a respectable air-fighter counterforce

and Soviet bombers, even such huge ones as the 'Blackjack' which is twenty-five per cent larger than the American B-1 and armoured, are unlikely to be able to penetrate NATO air-space very far or survive very long afterwards. They can launch missiles from great distances and heights but even with jamming and blinding they are at greater risk than any other Soviet or US missile-delivery system.

With the perfection and deployment of large space stations, conventional aeroplanes will probably continue to serve ground forces as transportation systems, for low-level tactical bombing and for little else, and presumably the admiration which once was lavished upon pilots will be shifted to spacemen.

In both the Soviet Union and the United States integration of air-space commands includes co-ordination of air arms and electronic space programmes. In the USSR and TRV (*Radioteknichskiye Voiska*) radio-technical command is responsbile for air-space electronic surveillance, operating space systems by co-ordinating these and a network of six thousand radar facilities with bomber command.

President Reagan approved of the creation of the American multi-service space command 'to co-ordinate defence efforts' including bomber command but the focus of strategy passed beyond bombers when physicists reached beyond gravity.

They are the new toymakers. They belong to a foreseeable future and as with computer technology their knowledge will not be limited to one country or to an international scientific community. Nor will it be hindered by 'limitation talks'. Space exploration will become the preserve of scientists but its exploitation for military purposes will become the playground of the new toymakers, those who develop sophisticated systems for ICBM deliveries.

This sophistication presently exists in only two countries, the US and the USSR, but the development of nuclear warheads without sophisticated delivery systems – which is the foundation of the entire fission-fusion idea; nuclear bombs by themselves – rests upon a different foundation. A dozen countries with enemies do not require sophisticated delivery systems, just the nuclear bombs: Iran and Iraq, for example, or Israel and Syria, Libya and Egypt, Turkey and Greece. Instead of a Volkswagen bus loaded with conventional explosives being driven into someone's barracks or embassy compound to kill several hundred people, a nuclear device delivered by a Volkswagen could kill thousands and destroy a city.

One of the ironies to arise from the US-USSR confrontation was demonstrated by conference scheduled for 28 November 1984 in Moscow where the nuclear powers could share their concern over proliferation of nuclear bombs. For nearly twenty years it had been possible to limit nuclear knowledge to five nations, the US, the USSR, Britain, France and China. Presently there is evidence that another four nations are capable of manufacturing nuclear weapons: Pakistan, India, Israel and South Africa. Four additional nations will be able to within ten years: Libya, Iraq, Brazil and Argentina. There is also evidence that at least one secret project to produce a nuclear bomb funded by Libya's Colonel Qaddafi and under the direction of a noted German scientist is being pushed as a private-sector enterprise.

The participants at the Moscow conference had reason for concern. The Carnegie Endowment for International Peace has warned that in 1983 eight nations with nuclear aspirations 'took important steps toward building or expanding nuclear-weapons capabilities'.

In 1968 120 signatories gave purpose to the Nuclear Proliferation Treaty which pledged that the three foremost nuclear powers at that time, the US, Britain and Soviet Union, would not give others the technology to make nuclear weapons. Two nations did not take the pledge, France and China. Since then both countries have made the technology available to other nations.

That was one cause for anxiety. Another had to do with the ease with which private companies have been able to avoid export controls in order to sell prohibited nuclear material. In this case an illegal nuclear pipeline was sharing with the illegal Intelligence pipeline a cornucopia of profits.

In 1984 a US government authority said that these aspiring countries 'are using dummy corporations, intermediaries, theft, anything they can to get hold of prohibited material'. It appeared that, while the superpowers were concentrating on their roles as nuclear and space adversaries, someone had left the back door open.

How easily this could result in a frightening situation was demonstrated in 1983 by Argentina's announcement that it had a plant in operation that could produce highly enriched uranium suitable for nuclear weapons. Production was estimated as sufficient to manufacture enough fissionable material for six bombs a year. This plant was built without outsiders knowing anything about it. That kind of secrecy could be extended to sales of production to non-nuclear nations with aspirations.

Iran has had German help in creating a nuclear-bomb capability. Libya offered Belgian scientists and engineers $1 million to help in the construction of two nuclear reactors. Iraq courted French assistance toward the same goal. Even South Korea has a nuclear programme. In 1983 US Intelligence services sent out a hundred 'nuclear-export alerts' about illegal transactions.

Nuclear technology is no more containable than was computer technology or than directed-energy R&D will be. Nor does it help that, with the superpowers loaded down with huge nuclear missiles, the trend now is toward improved smaller warheads. That will make counting them impossible. For example, the US Midgetman missile is an antithesis of the large US Minuteman missile and the huge MX Peacekeeper. Minuteman III has a throw-weight of 1,134 kilograms (2,500 pounds). MX's throw-weight is 3,765 kilograms (8,300 pounds). Midgetman's throw-weight is 454 kilograms (1000 pounds). Nor do Midgetmen missiles require the expensive housing required by large ICBMs. Because the cost of producing Midgetmen ICBMs would be less, more could be bought, and although small ICBMs have only one warhead, with more of them the net result would be the same. Also, Midgetmen can be made mobile very easily. It would be very difficult to destroy any significant number of them in a pre-emptive attack. All of these things have made them attractive to US planners. It makes them attractive to others as well, plus one additional advantage: they can be stolen very easily.

But the real toymaker's delight is the cruise missile. It is even smaller. It is also inexpensive to manufacture and very versatile; anyone can launch one: no elaborate delivery system is necessary, although to get the best performance out of their versatility they should be launched from the sea or the air. But armed with a nuclear warhead they will function admirably from fairly simple ground-launchers in Baghdad, Benghazi, Havana, a PLO camp in Lebanon or, with ingenuity, the bed of a small pickup truck. And because they are quite small they can be stolen easily and with any kind of luck in large numbers.

The cruise missile is the grandson of Germany's World War II 'buzz-bombs', V1 and V2 series. The V1 was a flying bomb delivered by a pulse-jet engine. It was vulnerable to ground-fire and warplane attack. The V2 was a ballistic missile against which no defence proved adequate. Cruise missiles are similar to drone aircraft, small and reliable. They are air-breathing, have an extensive range and in great numbers would be difficult to destroy on their way to a target even though they are not very fast. They fly very close to the ground, making them difficult to detect by radar and to destroy by ground fire. Present varieties are greatly improved over their V-series German predecessors. They are small enough to be carried in pods, and unless someone were to volunteer how many they possessed, there would be no way to know – obviously that is an unresolvable problem for either negotiators or military planners whose purposes are either to formulate a workable limitation or to devise an adequate defence.

There are three kinds of cruise missiles: ground-, air-, and sea-launched. Those presently based in NATO countries are ground-launched (GLCMs) but the original concept was for sea-launching (SLCR), and by about 1982 the air-launched (ALCM) cruise missile was developed. Initial experimentation included launching the missiles from ship-board but, surface vessels being vulnerable to aerial observation, SLCMs became part of the arsenal of attack-submarines. With submarines as delivery systems, cruise missiles could be launched from beneath the sea or carried close to shore-lines and launched from either on the surface or beneath it.

Aside from their appealing versatility and low cost, cruise missiles can be manufactured in great numbers in secret. They do not require the huge pads, silos and launchers large ICBMs need, and with improvement they have become quite sophisticated. Powered with fuel-efficient small propulsion engines, they have the ability to travel considerable distances, but what has made them particularly valuable is their TERCOM navigational system which uses a computer 'brain' to guide the missile over uneven terrain.

The TERCOM acronym is derived from 'terrain counter-matching'. The system translates terrain mapped by satellites into a code of digital numbers. The missile's radar is oriented downward toward the ground. Hills, lakes, forests and roads that appeared as pictures to the satellite but which were coded into numbers for the missiles are matched by the computer 'intelligence' so that as the ground-hugging cruise missile approaches a hill or a forest the 'brain' tells the guidance system to gain altitude. Afterward the 'brain' tells the guidance system to get back close to the ground.

Both the inertial guidance system and the power plant are adaptable to almost any military use. All cruise missiles function in an identical fashion whether air-, sea or ground-launched. From an aerial launch the missile can drop to within 15.2 metres (50 feet) of the ground and using its 'brain' fly around defensive obstacles, get below radar and at a speed of about 885 kilometres (550 miles) an hour manoeuvre according to a pre-scheduled time-setting to a target. TERCOM enables the missile to make guidance corrections *en route* in order to reach a target with a probability of error of one part to ten million. During its approach it can make corrections so as to approach from any direction.

Sea-launched cruise missiles (SLCMs) as well as GLCMs are shot out of launchers using a solid-propellant rocket. Fourteen seconds after the launch the missile's control systems and wings lock into operational position. Cruise missiles, in fact all ballistic missiles, share an identical problem: they cannot be called back. Bombers can, but if through accident, inadvertence or miscalculation an ICBM is launched, there is no way to recall it.

The US probably has as many as 15,000 cruise missiles. The Soviet Union inaugurated a cruise-missile programme earlier, not long after Russian troops came across V2 sites complete with prototypes and specifications in Germany during the Second World War. They began building them almost immediately. In estimating how many they have, any number can play.

During 1977 a US Joint Cruise Missile Project was established as part of DOD – Department of Defence – to co-ordinate production of the missiles and to keep track of them. At that time the 'Tomahawk' sea- and ground-launched missile was being manufactured by the General Dynamics Company while Boeing Aircraft Company produced a cruise missile for aerial launching. Since then thousands of them have been manufactured, nearly all with nuclear-capable warheads. Some became ICBMs when B-52 bombers became delivery systems because an increasingly invulnerable 'layered' Soviet system of defence made penetration by large US military aircraft of Russian air space unlikely. The B-52G would carry twelve ALCMs, and the B-52H would carry twenty. With 104 B-52Gs and 96 B-52Hs in the programme, the number of cruise missiles which could be fired at a target almost 3,218 kilometres (2,000 miles) distant was in the neighbourhood of three thousand.

However, the cruise missile is not infallible, as the recent Soviet embarrassment demonstrated when one of theirs went blithely into Scandinavia.

In the past they were dependable because they were uncomplicated. Sophistication has made them occasionally temperamental; their guidance and 'intelligence' systems have caused trouble. Presently, because there are so many, a duplication of the Soviet embarrassment can be expected. If an erring cruise missile is armed – that is, has a nuclear warhead, the result may be more than just embarrassing.

Also, Western technicians have been experimenting with false landscapes to confuse the TERCOM system, and travelling at about 885 kilometres (550 miles) an hour they are not fast enough to elude a good system of defence oriented toward detecting and destroying them. But because they are usually reliable, inexpensive and easily transported

in trucks or small boats and can be armed and launched
by relatively inexperienced technicians, Iraq could depopulate Iran very handily if it had enough of them, or
Hafez Assad could vaporize most of Israel's population.

What has contributed to the number of cruise missiles
aside from their negligible cost in relation to other ICBMs
and their versatility is that they have not been included in
limitation discussions – which may be reasonable: if they
cannot be found, they cannot be counted.

There may be as many as thirty thousand cruise missiles
in the world. That may be a low estimate. They can be
manufactured by anyone with a modern factory, knowledgeable hired help and the funds to promote production.

17
The High Frontier

An aggressive Soviet R&D programme aimed at developing technologies applicable to directed energy armament began in the 1960s, much earlier than similar US programmes, and presently USSR development is well ahead in areas of adequate power sources and high-quality optics.

One advantage of their head start has been to provide the Russians with sufficient knowledge to develop high-power microwave and millimetre-wave radio frequency weapons. Such systems could destroy electronic satellites and if used against manned space stations could harm astronauts.

Soviet research aimed at producing destructive particle-beam weapons is probably no more advanced than similar progress in the West, and in fact may not be as advanced. In both cases the deployment of such weapons is not envisioned before the late 1990s, although given the state of urgency this kind of technology had thrust upon it by the SDI proposal, earlier deployment is not impossible.

But the problems are significant, and the presentation of new concepts has emphasized the difficulties. A complete space-based ballistic missile defence programme includes a number of different systems. The easiest part may be accomplishing co-ordination among them to protect populations while simultaneously defending military areas.

As presently conceived they would eliminate a majority of hostile warheads and do it without using nuclear force, and as with most novelties, 'authorities' have appeared with the abandon of autumn leaves.

A Washington-based organization call 'High Frontier' made up largely of scientists and retired generals was one example. High Frontier offered a proposal based on weapons to provide a global defence which would put into orbit individual vehicles carrying about forty-five small attack modes. Each of the 432 vehicles would orbit 300 nautical miles about Earth inclined 65 degrees to the equator so as to cover most of the Soviet Union's landmasses. Each armed attack mode aboard the individual delivery vehicles would be fitted with a rocket to enable acceleration to one kilometre (0.621 mile) per second. Modes would collide with targets under great impact before the ICBMs were far enough into their launch for internal mechanisms to activate their warheads.

The idea was to ram Soviet ICBMs in their initial boost stage. Assuming seventeen thousand modes would make the attack and the number of ICBMs to be attacked would be in the neighbourhood of two thousand, even assuming an equal number of decoy ICBMs were simultaneously launched, the ratio of destruction should be satisfactory.

The High Frontier proposal also advocated two additional identical systems in space between the USSR and the US to attack and destroy the ICBMs which survived the first attack. To defend US missile silos it was suggested that as many as ten thousand modes travelling on an intercepting course at 1.5 kilometres (0.9 miles) per second would destroy any ICBMs which got past the other systems.

Subsequently part of the High Frontier proposal was modified. Instead of ten thousand expensive modes, silo-defence would be accomplished by firing a wall of bullet-type projectiles from the ground. A Soviet ASAT which destroyed a target satellite in one experiment operated on a similar principle; it riddled the target with dozens of small pellets.

The High Frontier proposal was based on the need for the West to be able to cope with a Soviet pre-emptive strike before SDI technology was able to develop an operational defence. It suggested that the system could be produced quickly from hardware already at hand. To support this view the proposal said that, 'While significant beam weapons capabilities have been demonstrated in the laboratory, their deployment in global defence systems is too far in the future to meet the urgencies of the High Frontier study.'

Critics made three points. One was that the High Frontier cost estimate was unrealistic. Figured to cost $24 billion over a five-year period with another $40 billion later, the actual cost would be closer to $200 billion in initial stages with more later. The second point was that the High Frontier projection of a system that could be operational within a few years was also unrealistic; it would require at least a decade, roughly the same length of time the SDI concepts would require. The third point was that, with the ability the Soviet Union presently has to destroy space vehicles through its advanced ASAT systems, they could eliminate the delivery vehicles before their attack modes could be launched. Even without using ASATs, there is evidence the Soviets could use advanced high-power microwave and millimetre-wave radio frequency weapons to accomplish the same purpose.

Basically the High Frontier concept went back to a project called 'Bambi' in the early 1960s, and since then such proposals as the Strategic Defence Initiative have not simply progressed past the stage of something like a Gatling gun firing swarms of bullets but have travelled in different directions. For example, the current trend is to duplicate the Soviet manned orbital space station, putting technicians aloft, not to concentrate on High-Frontier-type ground-launched and controlled small vehicles. Toward that end the US trained its initial cadre of military astronauts to supervise space-shuttle flights concerned with military missions. A classified Defence Department project included putting twenty-seven military astronauts, trained in secret by the Air Force, aboard the shuttle *Discovery* in 1985 to conduct defence experiments. For the first time military personnel were to play a dominant role in the US manned space programme.

Presently, recruiting is among all four services. The number of men in training is small, nor in all probability will it escalate even assuming space stations large enough to accommodate a hundred astronauts will eventually appear, so the current anxiety about space armies, at least into the foreseeable future, is premature.

One hundred specialists could perform the functions necessary for the prosecution of space conflict, which has almost nothing in common with massed tactical advances into an enemy's territory on Earth. Even a dozen manned stations would not require an 'army' to operate them, and barring the huge space stations as imagined in science fiction, which are not presently feasible and could not be put into orbit given the current state of technology, a future war in space would be conducted by comparatively very small numbers of specialists. At present it is not practical even to build such a station, certainly not in the US where the newly formed military space command to co-ordinate extra-terrestrial efforts is subject to approval for funding for multi-billion-dollar research over the next ten years to develop a war-fighting capability in space using lasers, particle-beam weapons and high-velocity 'railguns' to fire projectiles at speeds measured in miles per second, which are improbable enough. A huge experimental space station which could not be lifted off the ground would get nothing.

Between 1985 and 1989 small groups of military astronauts called 'payload specialists' by the DOD are to supervise sixteen shuttle flights, and no one anticipates more than a minimum manpower requirement even though the US space shuttle programme is to be expanded. With the advent of the SDI project, shuttles which have heretofore been exclusively for civilian scientific use will become the workhorses of America's space-defence system. They will implement methods for protecting satellites such as hardening them against radiation effects of nuclear explosions and making them less vulnerable to electronic blinding and jamming. They will also enhance them so that they will be capable of taking evasive action.

Because these space assets are critical to defence and at the same time likely to be destroyed at the outbreak of hostilities, DOD shuttle technicians will also launch 'cold bird' satellites. These are to remain undetected in very high orbit as replacements, silent and invisible until needed, then moved to lower space and activated.

An analyst of the International Peace Research Institute at Stockholm, Sweden, said that, 'Talk about the dangers of extending the arms race to space is a bit of a myth. What is not generally appreciated is the extent and speed with which outer space has been put to military use.'

Emphasizing this point, the Soviet Union in a co-ordinated exercise launched two ICBMs, one from a submarine and two anti-ballistic-missile rockets to track and destroy the ICBMs in a practice attack upon space weapons.

As the Stockholm analyst noted, the High Frontier had become a military preserve. In the 1990s, according to a US Major-General, John Storrie, chief of the Air Force's Space Directorate, 'It will be necessary to put up satellites armed with lasers, or some other kind of weapons ... The technology is there. It is just a matter of committing the resources to get it done.' Not quite. 'Committing the resources' means massive funding, but smothering scientists with greenbacks will not provide them with knowledge they do not have. In experiments with an airborne laser system installed in a gutted Boeing 707, the Air Force tracked and destroyed Sidewinder air-to-air missiles and cruise-missile drones flying barely above the surface of the Pacific Ocean. Louis Marquet, previously quoted, has said that 'People have a hard time accepting the idea that lasers can kill at a distance, but we now have the ability to burn holes in chunks of steel at a very great distance.'

But not in space. Robert Cooper, Director of DARPA, suggests that the US will perhaps be able to deploy directed-energy anti-satellite weapons some time in the 1990s, probably chemical lasers that could be put into orbit. By the year 2000, so the theory goes, ASAT lasers could be fired from Earth to hit huge orbiting reflector-mirrors previously put into space from shuttles.

The difference between enthusiasm and fact is probably the same as it is between cruise drones skimming over the ocean at wave-level and the nearest low-orbit satellite in space. 'Committing the resources' in this case means DOD's plan to spend over $5 billion a year over the next five years on directed-energy research as part of President Reagan's $26 billion Strategic Defence Initiative development programme.

There will certainly be advances. There will be room for them in the future as there has in the past as science and technology progressed toward what is currently states-of-the-art, but the technology does not now exist in the US to

destroy satellites in space from laser facilities on the ground
nor does it appear likely that in its entirety the SDI concept
will achieve its goals before the year 2000, if then.

In the laser category the Soviet Union is well ahead. A
ground-based laser system at Sary Shagan in the southern
USSR is presently capable of damaging some varieties of
satellites.

In its drive for eminence DOD programmes called the
'Triad', a series of interacting research projects, are
hastening to create laser weapons. One of these projects,
called 'Alpha', is engaged in the development of a
small-energy chemical laser. Another called 'Lode', an
acronym for Large Optics Demonstration Experiment, is
involved with perfecting mirrors that could be used to aim a
laser beam in space. The Triad's third undertaking, called
Talon Gold, has as its goal an upgraded system for locating
and tracking satellites.

There is also a separate project called Teal Ruby. Its
purpose is to perfect infra-red sensors which while operating
in space would detect low-flying aircraft and ground-
hugging cruise missiles whose locations, courses and rates of
speed could be transmitted to space-based lasers.

Another project, this one perhaps likely to catch the
popular imagination because little has been disclosed about
it, is the electromagnetic railgun. It transforms electrical
force into propulsion pressure to fire small projectiles at
velocities that measure their distance in miles per second,
many times faster than conventional firearms – 1,448
kilometres (900 miles) a minute. As a system to protect
satellites in space by blowing away hostile ASATs, railguns
are practical and can be produced soon. But designing their
delivery system may delay deployment. Nevertheless, DOD
must view them as a near-term asset because in 1984 it
allocated $35 million to the railgun research and develop-
ment project.

There are other projects, mostly classified, whose goal is to
hasten and increase the effectiveness – or the attractiveness –
of President Reagan's SDI Star Wars programme. The ones
currently available for study through public domain have
certainly reached the USSR through subscriptions to such

periodicals as *Aviation Weekly and Space Technology*, an outstanding publication in its field. Perhaps too, moles and merchants are presently in process of sending specifications and progress reports eastward through the clandestine pipeline. Certainly the SDI project is well underway and of critical concern to the Soviet Union.

It is the first genuinely new Western defence proposal in twenty years. It has appeal, primarily one may assume because, as President Reagan has said, 'The awesome destructive potential of nuclear weapons [requires] that we must seek ... means for deterring war. It is both militarily and morally necessary.'

But in the background of logistical eulogies an occasional reference to $35 million, $24 billion, $3.7 billion and $21 billion appears to support a contention of Reginald Turnill, editor of *Jane's Spaceflight Directory*, that, 'The battle for space-based laser weapons is settling down to be grimmer and much more expensive than the race to the moon twenty years ago.' How expensive it may be to seek a genuine defensive shield, let alone create one, if one can be created, does not appear to be amenable to specifics. Nor do hypothesists seem to welcome ideas for defence that do not require lyrical arithmetical dollar-formulae.

Microwave weapons sources are less expensive than lasers, for example. One-thousand-watt microwave tubes in quantities could be manufactured for about $50 each. Power from a large infra-red carbon-dioxide laser costs about that much for each of the thousand watts.

There is evidence that, before upwards of $5 billion a year exclusively for directed-energy research is spent, attention might be accorded a number of scientists who share an opinion that it would be cheaper and more practical to develop mirrors for use on space assets which would defend them against laser attack by reflecting light beams elsewhere. This would not resolve the problem of enemy lasers but it would blunt their effectiveness, leaving their destruction to other systems. Or in the most euphoric view, if inexpensive shields proved effective and were used on all items requiring defence, what would be the point in either side continuing to develop, or to deploy, ruinously expensive directed-energy systems?

Optimism and costs aside, there exists a large and divergent sector of opposition to the Star Wars concept. Arms-control advocates see even basic research as a peril to international relations. The Union of Concerned Scientists offered an opinion to the effect that even 'The effort to build and deploy these defensive technologies could spur a dangerous phase of the arms race. Insurmountable technological and political obstacles will prevent us from developing an effective shield against nuclear weapons.' True as this may be, it ignores the fact that such an arms race has been in progress for twenty years. It also overlooks recent trends toward employing non-nuclear systems of defence against nuclear attack, and finally, now that space has become the new frontier, neither side is likely to abandon it.

Europeans too are sceptics. It must be said that they always have been, for while appearing to desire US protection, expecting it as a matter of course, they prefer to avoid sharing in many of the sacrifices mutual protection requires while at the same time offering perennial criticism. For years NATO members expected the US to bear the heaviest burden for tactical protection; at the same time some of them were unconvinced that deploying US cruise and Pershing missiles served their national interests. Somehow the US commitment to defend Europe, Australia and New Zealand was to be accomplished by the US unilaterally.

Australia agreed to allow the US to use its air bases to monitor MX-missile tests, then reneged. New Zealand closed its ports to US warships that might be carrying nuclear weapons, evidently oblivious to the fact that US warships would only be that far from home as part of an extensive defensive exercise in that part of the world. They want protection but from the middle of the road.

This niggling contentiousness is only the most recent example of NATO's lack of vitality for collective action. The argument which has been raised perennially by America's allies, particularly the Europeans, that they are closer to the USSR and are therefore in more imminent peril has had no validity since Russian armies overran Germany. Fifty years later Soviet missiles can reach the US in thirty minutes. No one is closer or farther from the peril than anyone else. The fear of a holocaust hangs over everyone, everywhere, equally.

It appears the US has allied itself with nations who not only are suspicious of its intentions and fearful of its strategic defence policies but have self-serving leaders who listen to minorities of dissenters and ignore the principle concerning the strength of unity as opposed to the disasters which have historically accompanied a lack of it.

Nevertheless, America's allies have some justification for their anxieties. US proponents of SDI have oversold their programme and uneasy Europeans have not been made less so by the number of qualified authorities who have come forth to say that President Reagan's vision of an impenetrable umbrella of defence is not possible. This kind of criticism has caused worry in the United States as well. Some of the critics say that the US is rushing headlong into an escalation of the arms race in pursuit of an unattainable goal.

Pragmatic Europeans would perhaps have been less sceptical of SDI had it been explained differently. As a system of defence it would have the capability of stopping between thirty and fifty per cent of Soviet missiles. Also, SDI can increase stability by strengthening deterrence. The SDI space-defence system, whose purpose would be to protect land-based missiles, might interject fresh uncertainty into the calculations of Soviet strategists who contemplate a first-strike attack against the US or its allies. The risk of failure would be unthinkable.

Those are the realistic virtues of SDI. It has been overselling the visionary dream of a world safe from nuclear war and its extension, a time when nuclear weapons would be outdated, that has heightened scepticism, increased the number of critics and undermined the obtainable objectives of the first original initiative as a replacement for the Mutual Assured Destruction philosophy.

Critics who point out that such an overall system of defence is far into the future have grounds for their conviction, although critics are not ordinarily taken into the

confidence of those engaged in classified projects. Space
stations, for example, as well as railguns and hardened
satellites, are not 'in the future' at all. But the total concept
is. George Keyworth, previously cited, President Reagan's
science adviser, has said that, 'We don't even yet have any
real idea what a system would look like,' and the Office of
Technology Assessment noted in 1984 that the prospect for
a functioning system is 'so remote that it should not serve as
the basis of public expectation nor national policy'.

Here the implication that national policy should not rely
on SDI sidesteps the fact that national policy does not rely
on it. Realistically it relies upon nuclear parity. The latest
indication of support for this was Congressional approval of
the MX-missile programme.

What the Strategic Defence Initiative offers is a method
for getting out of the Mutual Assured Destruction rut. Its
most unique characteristic is that by being available to both
sides it provides an opportunity for paranoid Russians and
worried people throughout the rest of the world to worry
less. Nevertheless, and regardless of widespread dissatis-
faction with the strategy of Mutual Assured Destruction, as
a basis for deterrence it has worked and is still working. It
certainly is not attractive and as a basis for survival it leaves
room for improvement, yet during the past forty years,
whether its philosphy has been morally tenable or not, it
has been a force for peace. As a 'balance of terror' it de-
parted from earlier deterrent strategy, where one nation
held greater war-making capability than another, by having
both superpowers equally as powerful.

In this instance the result has been what is referred to in
those literary gems which have been America's contribution to immortal literature, the 'Western' as 'a Mexican
stand-off'.

Especially objectionable about the MAD philosophy has
been the accepted conviction that there is no defence
against nuclear-missile attacks. A billion or two human
beings must die. For the previous forty years the human
condition has prevailed with varying degrees of discomfort
under that philosophy; now there is a possibility of something better – or is there?

18

Feasibility and Fact

President Reagan's 23 March 1983 announcement of the proposed Strategic Defence Initiative as successor to MAD touched off a fire storm of worldwide controversy. It caused pandemonium in the ranks of MAD proponents and brought forth a host of scientists whose conflicting views initiated and sustained an enormous amount of confusion.

Is it possible or is it not possible for technology to provide shields so that a billion or so human beings will not have to die? What is the implication of SDI technology toward the year 2000?

A number of sources, mainly those close to the current US national administration, have implied that the technology is at hand. In opposition are scientists who claim it is not at hand and that, even if it were theoretically feasible, development and deployment are far into the future.

The US Department of Defence's chief research organization, the Defence Advanced Research Projects Agency (DARPA), has established two bureaus of scientific enquiry, one to prove high-energy weapons are feasible, one to prove they are not. There is too much at stake, billions of dollars, thousands of man-hours, possibly millions of human lives, not to undertake some kind of critical evaluation.

As a concept SDI is an unparalled departure from earlier ideas of defence. As a new endeavour it has no precedents to rely upon and yet it is essential that the correct judgements be made because they will be important to everyone and could affect the entire international order of existence.

SDI blurs the traditional distinguishing elements between 'defence' and 'offence'. All weapons are classified as 'defensive' by those who own them. To those who are decimated by them they are 'offensive' weapons. With high-energy systems including those deployed to protect against incoming missiles the distinction is academic because laser, particle-beam and microwave transmissions designed to destroy missiles are also capable of cooking people – in theory.

Ideally, the kind of weapons envisioned in the SDI proposal should have shocking, maiming and killing power. They should be able to reach and disable targets on the ground or in the atmosphere, and do it so fast the target cannot escape. They should be reliable, not subject to malfunction, and capable of delivering enormous amounts of energy when it is required.

Conventional artillery pieces make a lot of noise, require constant maintenance and miss a lot, but they deliver lethal projectiles under great impact. Beam weapons not only lack impact but have other idiosyncrasies artillery pieces do not have. Their lethal energy can be diffused while passing through the atmosphere, and because they require great amounts of energy, provided at present by generators housed in stationary structures – some as large as a two-storey building, they cannot be moved from place to place. They do not possess shocking power. They can for example injure a tank's 'eyes' – its sensors – and make it very hot but they cannot roll it over.

High-energy lasers project a concentrated beam of light at 300,000 kilometres (186,420 miles) per second. Particle beams which project sub-atomic particles or atoms can operate nearly as fast, but the central question is whether either can be operated as a weapon over considerable distances, or accurately.

A laser capable of emitting two million watts of energy in a continuous beam has been developed, with the expectation that one of ten million watts can be built. In experiments lasers have destroyed aircraft and small missiles under controlled conditions, but not at great distances.

The term 'laser' – from 'light amplification by stimulated emission' – implies a simplification. A 'laser' is the weapon but the weapon is dependent upon a 'system'. The system is huge and almost immovable. Its purpose is to generate sufficient energy to create the laser beam. Not only is the system not easily moved but rarely are power sources readily available to supply the laser's requirements independently of the system.

In airborne tests lasers have performed satisfactorily and in one instance, where a large combat vehicle similar to a tank had a system installed in it, there was no room for anything else and in order to remove the system the vehicle had to be dismantled; nevertheless, at close range the laser performed well against thin metal. But these were tactical experiments and their range was not great. Presumably the problems could be overcome. But President Reagan's SDI proposal envisions high-energy defence miles above Earth, and this would require much larger and greatly enhanced systems. Someone has said that such a system would not have to be efficient, it could simply be dropped on the enemy.

There are range-finder lasers which are small and operate on a principle similar to radar. When directed toward a target, they reach it and return. This round trip is measurable so that both distance and location can be pinpointed for destruction by conventional ground weapons. This laser is not a weapon by itself any more than radar is a weapon.

In 1967 a 'gas-phase' laser was developed with continuous power-level requirements of up to sixty kilowatts – sixty thousand watts – and no sooner had this idea achieved manageable levels in the West than the USSR acquired the technology.

This 'gasdynamic' laser development made possible the creation of militarily significant lethal lasers. But these were not of 'Star Wars' quality, although in theory they provided some tantalizing possibilities. For example, a laser which projects a beam of controlled light at 299,274 kilometres (186,000 miles) a second could be aimed at a missile travelling at Mach 6 from a distance of 161 kilometres (100 miles) and reach the missile before it had travelled three metres (ten feet). But a laser consists of massless radiation photons, and by the time the beam reached the missile high overhead in flight, the laser would be hopelessly diffused. This problem is presently receiving intense study in the US.

A particle beam, on the other hand, has weight. Particle beams consist of streams of highly energized atomic or sub-atomic particles–electrons, photons, ions etc – which are less susceptible to diffusion in the atmosphere. But they have their own problems. One is that particle beams are affected by the Earth's magnetic field.

Both systems would destroy their targets in the same way, by striking missiles with high concentrations of energy, either charged particles or photons, which would impact on the missile and damage it physically or penetrate to its electronic viscera causing an electronic haemorrhage.

It is something like this which SDI advocates envision but the technology is illusive. Where the greatest present potential exists is not 3,200 kilometres (2,000 miles) above Earth, it is *on* Earth, even though the same fundamental problems exist there, diffusion and magnetic distraction, for example.

Battlefield tacticians are intrigued by directed-energy weapons at ground-level. A laser beam travelling at the speed of light would move forty thousand times faster than the swiftest rocket, which would eliminate the need to 'lead' a target, a prime reason for missing. In the one six-millionth of a second required for light to travel 1.609 kilometres (1 mile), the fastest jet aircraft travelling at twice the speed of sound would move slightly over 0.3175 mm (0.125 inches) one eighth of an inch. A laser could be aimed directly at its target to achieve satisfactory results. Even charged particles which do not achieve the speed of light, especially under normal outdoor, ground-level atmospheric conditions, move at 1,000 kilometres (621 miles) per second, which is still a thousand times faster than the swiftest jet aircraft, so 'leading' would not be necessary there either.

There are other enticements for tactical officers, and at least in their ground-level environment practical deployment is possible right now for some high-energy systems. If the problem of mobility can be overcome by the year 2000, it will be possible to 'fire' beam weapons at about two a second for particle beams and one 'shot' every two seconds with lasers, which should create problems for an enemy. However, this is largely theory, and even if beam weapons reach conventional battlefields, they will not replace artillery shells or even grenades. Beams travel in a straight line. They cannot for example cause the inconvenience of a grenade which can be lobbed through a doorway, around a corner or into a trench. Nor can they blow away a fortification or even the tree a solider has taken shelter behind. Nor, as has been noted, while they may be able to strike aircraft or vehicles, can they penetrate armour or achieve impact. What they *can* accomplish against armoured vehicles, most of which have electronic sighting or guidance systems, is to burn out sensors and short-circuit electronic systems, and this same capability can create havoc among soliders. Theoretically it would be possible to incinerate soldiers with intense microwave beams, but in order to accomplish this huge antennae would have to be erected and that would not be practical on a battlefield even if an enemy would allow them to be set up.

Particle beam could kill soldiers if they could reach them, but at ground-level particle beams would have difficulty with atmospheric conditions.

There is one way beam weapons could devastate battlefield personnel. The human eye is a sensor. It is very sensitive to light, as anyone knows who has stared at the sun. A laser beam projecting only several thousandths of a watt of visible light can permanently damage the retina, the fragile membrane at the rear of the eyeball that senses light and relays images to the brain. Depending upon the wavelength, power and duration of laser beams, eye-injury can be temporary, injurious but not blinding, or can result in permanent loss of sight. During the hostilities between Vietnam and China a few years ago, the Vietnamese used Soviet chemical lasers to blind Chinese soldiers. Perhaps as a result of these satisfactory results the Soviet Union has since then engaged in extensive anti-personnel laser-blinding experiments.

That laser range-finder mentioned earlier (page 205) can cause eye-damage if a soldier is standing directly in line when the beam is aimed for purposes of locating and targeting an object, even though that is not the specific objective in aiming the device.The natural reflex of blinking when bright light reaches the eye, nature's way of providing protection against normal brilliance, is also triggered by the pain caused by a laser or infra-red pulse of brilliance, but if an intense, short pulse lasting no more than one ten-millionth of a second strikes the eye, it can cause damage before the blinking reflex can be completed. The blinding light of an exploding artillery shell causes temporary vision problems but, if the explosion is close enough, permanent injury will probably be to the eardrums not the eyes.

Granting that directed-energy weapons have a potential for achieving ends conventional weapons cannot and granting they will be used on up-coming battlefields, there are about as many things they cannot do as there are that they may be able to do. They cannot achieve the versatility of hand-held weapons. They cannot be made to pistol-size. If they were, they would be too hot to hold. Nor can they destroy targets on Earth from aloft such as being aimed from a space station. They are not capable of causing the mass destruction nuclear missiles or conventional bombs can cause, and defence against them involves little more than avoiding direct confrontation. These are the facts. The feasibilities and theories suggest otherwise but at the present state of technology moving from theory to deployment is only marginally possible and in some cases not possible at all. In cases where progress is being made, actual practical development of workable systems is a long way into the future. Particle beams have problems of more complexity than lasers, and microwaves or infra-red systems while theoretically attractive as weapons have limitations which may very well prevent their ever being developed as weapons.

This does not mean high-energy weapons will not be deployable by the year 2000; it means that all phases of directed energy will not. High energy is a force; some of it is amenable to control and direction. President Reagan's vision of a directed-energy shield against Soviet missiles has two elements in its favour. One is speed. If directed-energy beams can be propagated to eliminate at least most of the diffusion they waste in transit and can be 'bounced' off huge space-reflectors into the path of on-coming missiles with sufficient intensity to cause damage, they should be able to provide protection because they travel much faster than the missiles and could zap them miles short of their targets. The second favourable element is that, given the intensity of present research, spurred by the President's proposal, the gap between feasibility and fact could be significantly shortened because, even though current problems are immense, they are not beyond understanding. For example, lasers are inefficient in transposing fed-in power into beams of directed energy, but reflectors have been employed to redirect energy into efficient concentrations of light, after techniques were discovered to increase more efficient methods of translating power.

At present research is being pushed to resolve the problem of diffusion over great distances – into space, for instance. The farther beams are sent from Earth, the weaker – more diffused – they become. They can be controlled over short distances; this has been demonstrated many times. Present research along lines which would employ the physics of short-distance projection to direct controlled beams into space using the known technology will probably provide an answer for aiming controlled lasers into space by the year 2000, if not earlier.

Experiments with 'mirrors' have progressed satisfactorily too; not only can controlled lasers be reflected in different directions for aiming purposes, but prismatic mirrors pick up and re-intensify the beam in much the same way that a magnifying glass catches sunlight and sets paper afire. The difficulty arises from the fact that distances are likely to be very great in space. In order to position a suitable mirror up there which would be large enough to gather and concentrate lethal beams over a considerable distance, the mirror would have to be huge, at least in its assembled state. Presently there is no way to get it up there in one piece. It could conceivably be taken up unassembled and put together by technicians.

The alternative is to put the entire beam-system into space. That technology is at hand – the space shuttles, for example. By pushing to the limit, such a system could probably be developed but it would have its inherent limitations intact. Mainly, it would be huge, heavier than anything ever put into space, and while this is not seen as an insurmountable difficulty and in fact may not be – when the first experimental small, lightweight weather satellite was lofted, no one knew how to put a space station up there; now they do – re-designing a laser system to be small and lightweight and not sacrifice the lethal purpose of the beam requires a lot more than simply substituting aluminium for steel: it involves problems in physics which cannot be resolved overnight.

In laboratory tests it has been possible to concentrate a particle beam upon a metal disc one metre (3.28 feet) thick and burn a hole two-thirds of the way through it. In order to accomplish this, the disc was fixed in place, the beam was close and the concentration of light was dialled down to pencil-size. Assuming the beam from a space station were reduced to the same lethal diameter, in order to damage a nuclear missile travelling at Mach 6, hitting the target with a pencil-sized beam would be difficult, and holding it steadily in one place long enough for it to burn a hole in the hull or to overheat the electronic systems seems to be asking a lot of credibility, particularly since light beams in space are invisible.

Also, beams – lasers more than particle beams, being vulnerable to the atmosphere, could encounter difficulties even if an enemy did not devise countermeasures. Normal fog would inhibit a laser; the tiny droplets of water scatter light – hence 'grey', foggy days. Rain, snow, haze, cloud-cover: each creates problems. Beams could burn through but their effectiveness would be impaired, particularly at any distance. Experiments with heat beams to dissipate fog have been satisfactory but not on a large scale, and an effective countermeasure is 'fog oil' created by burning diesel oil under conditions that cause excessive smoke and light-refracting fumes.

These are some of the problems at ground-level. In space the enduring cloud-cover above Earth would create the same problem as fog on Earth. Also, for deployment in space the system would be made lighter and smaller; at the present time the smaller the system, the less effective the beam.

It is possible to make X-ray lasers that are potentially lethal, but X-ray lasers do not travel well in the atmosphere, and in order to activate one it would require an explosion of considerable force because their activation threshold is very high.

Beyond the atmosphere it is feasible to intercept missiles, to wage a furious war of crackling lights and exploding targets, but on Earth, even if the fall-out reached down that far, there would be minimal danger. The same shield that protects Earth from dangerous sunlight radiation would protect it from this man-made peril – the atmosphere. The atmosphere absorbs heat and bends light. The higher a transmitted beam, the higher atmospheric resistance. Lasers aimed at Earth from space would probably not reach that far and if they did would be harmless by the time they got there.

It is possible that a beam could be developed that would detonate ammunition stores, as occurred on the Kola Peninsula, or ignite the invisible vapours which surround some kinds of chemical, oil and gasoline facilities, especially those where great amounts are stored, by maintaining a high level of heat from a laser in space over a period of time. However, a simple countermeasure for protection would require a reflector surface to 'bounce back' the beam, and for this purpose a relatively inexpensive shield of aluminium should be adequate.

Soviet theorists appear to believe that space-based particle generators aimed toward Earth could transfer particles to atoms and molecules in the atmosphere causing a shower of radiation on Earth. However, to kill people this way would require a weapon system capable of producing ten billion watts for an hour or an even greater force for shorter periods of time, and into the foreseeable future there is no way such a system could be developed. Even if it were possible, the cost would be much greater than the cost of nuclear bombs which can kill people in greater numbers and more efficiently.

The kinds of lasers currently under study include low- and high-energy lasers, carbon-dioxide lasers, gas dynamic, carbon-monoxide, chemical-oxygen, short-wavelength,

X-ray, excimer and free-electron lasers, along with variations employing the systems and requirements of basic lasers. Two classifications help eliminate the confusion of too many kinds: 'eudoatmospheric' lasers, for use in the atmosphere, and 'exo-atmospheric' lasers, for use in outer space. Exoatmospheric lasers to provide a protective shield are what SDI is all about. Ex at.nospheric lasers travelling at the speed of light should be able to reach a target instantaneously and provide an umbrella of protection for free-world nations, and they can, but, because in the atmosphere absorption dissipation and distortion would for practical purposes make a beam ineffective if it had to travel any distance, they will not provide an umbrella of defence very soon.

In outer space, where there are no such distractions, the chances for success are greater – at least space is less hostile; nevertheless, ground-based lasers projecting their beams to mirrors in space would have problems of which the atmosphere would be only one.

Mirrors for a five-million-watt chemical laser would be about four metres (thirteen feet), in size. For a ten-million-watt laser a forty-metre- (thirty-three-feet) mirror would be required. To build such reflectors and get them into space is presently getting considerable attention in the US. At least four defence-oriented companies are prepared to build prototypes. One company, United Technologies Research, proposed a mirror not of glass or shiny metal but of graphite fibre strengthened with glass for the frame which would be lightweight hence easier to get up there, with a reflector made of a vaporized silicon coating. The US National Aeronautics and Space Agency (NASA) proposed a thirty-metre, (one hundred-feet) mirror for use with large lasers. Another proposal, with an eye to the difficulty of lifting anything large in one piece, offered an inflatable mirror. The reflectors can be built and the high-energy systems are being developed. The idea is to 'fire' from the ground to the mirror with the beam reflected from the mirror to an incoming satellite or nuclear missile.

Obviously without its reflector the system would be useless and just as obviously an enemy would have laser mirrors as top-priority items for destruction. In fact, at the present time it is possible for the newer, more sophisticated ASATs to find a reflector and destroy it.

Another problem in space would be fire-control systems. There has to be some variety of information-processing component to co-ordinate the various functions of a laser system. In other words a computer. At present there is no computer which can, for example, identify hostile missiles, or satellites, unless they conform to recognizable profiles. An enemy who has the same or similar computers and knows how this works could develop a countermeasure. For example, a Soviet missile's recognizable characteristics can be altered to match the recognizable characteristics of a US missile. Further, the requirement for speed at aiming in space would be hindered because, although energy beams travel at the speed of light, the computer brains in their systems cannot co-ordinate information anywhere nearly that fast. Also, computers capable of directing fire-control systems requiring instantaneous adjustments of mirrors thousands of times a second do not exist.

It seems that the problems associated with high-energy technology involve resolving one difficulty and then being confronted with several new ones. Progess has been made and will continue to be made but which theoretical beam weapons will eventually become actual weapons is anyone's guess.

X-ray lasers may fall by the wayside because, regardless of what else may make them attractive, to activate them requires something like a small nuclear bomb. It is not this requirement which makes X-ray lasers undersirable to weapon-developers. It is the bomb itself. Of the interminable arms-limitation discussions which have taken place over the years, some of which have resulted in treaties, detecting the violations of nuclear clauses has been possible through satellite detection. The same sky-spies would pick up the detonation of an X-ray triggering device. Otherwise laser systems in process of development in US and USSR laboratories are impossible to detect from above. This adds to the suspicions of adversaries. If it cannot be verified what the other side is doing, what progress is being made, regardless of treaties there is no incentive for either side to limit development programmes.

With ICBMs simple deployment offered visible evidence of what each side owned, and deductions made from sky-spy photography permitted analysts to identify missiles according to classifications. Presently, deployment of high-energy beam systems would be equally as identifiable from the sky, but unlike nuclear missiles the thrust of high-energy R&D has been to make the systems smaller while at the same time increasing their lethality. When this occurs, a beam system will be easily transported, or hidden, thus difficult to detect.

What in fact seems likely is that both the US and the USSR will pursue policies of discussion while simultaneously striving to achieve overlordship of space, and within the next two decades one side or the other will stake it out as an extension of the national soil, accomplishing this as a posture not so much of superiority as of menace because regardless of an assortment of almost infinite technical difficulties, by the year 2000 it will be feasible to produce and deploy a beam system which will provide some degree of protection against ICBMs.

What shape this system may take defies present definition. The technical factors have yet to be comprehensively explored. What appears evident is that the Strategic Defence Initiative has taken the arms race to new levels. If as its critics contend it cannot perform as the US President expects, neither will it be the expensive mistake they predict.

Some aspects of it are presently realistic. Some have already become operational. Still others are in process of becoming operational.

About two-thirds of the total concept is not technologically feasible at the present time but, having been provided with ample financial support and political encouragement, by the year 2000 it is entirely possible the SDI shield against Soviet hardware will exist, and that impinges upon a question for the next generation: who owns space?

Bibliography

National Suicide, Military Aid to the Soviet Union, by Antony C. Sutton (Arlington House, New York)

Soviet Military Power (1983, 1984, 1985, a US government compilation of information; Washington, DC)

Realism, Strength, Negotiation (the US Department of State, Bureau of Public Affairs, Washington, DC, 1984)

Soviet Acquisition of Western Technology (a US government summary from various federal sources including the Intelligence and diplomatic agencies; Washington, DC)

The Secret War, Sanche de Gramont, G.P. Putnam's Sons, New York.

The Service, General Reinhard Gehlen, World Publishing Company, New York.

A History of Soviet and Russian Sea Power D.W. Mitchell, McMillan Publishing Company, New York and London.

The Atmosphere, Anthes, Panofsky, Cahr and Range, Charles E. Merrill Company, Ohio.

The Weather, Ti Sanders, Icarus Press, Indiana.

Soviet Active Measures, Hearings Before the Permanent Select Committee on Intelligence, US House of Representatives, Ninety-Seventh Congress, 13 and 14 July 1982 US government, Washington, DC.

Laser, Hecht and Teresi, Ticknor & Fields, New York.

Massacre 007 Richard Rohmer, Hodder & Stoughton, London.

Fundamentals of Electronics, volumes 1 through 8, compiled by the US Bureau of Naval Personnel, Washington, DC.

Lasers, Bela Lengyel, John Wiley & Sons, London.

Essentials of Lasers, L. Allen, Pergamon Books, London.

Robots and Think Machines, Julian May, Garden City Books, New York.

Silicon Chips and You, E.D. Renmore, Beaufort Books Incorporated, New York.

Robotics on Your Doorstep, Winkless and Bruning, Robotics Press, Portland, Oregon.

Here Comes the Robots, Joyce Milton, Hastings House Publishers, New York.

Additional sources include verifiable media information, correspondence and conversations, Intelligence reports and analytical evaluations, plus NATO publications and documents made available to the public by US and foreign governments.

Finally, *The Enchanted Loom*, by Robert Jastrow, published by Simon & Schuster of New York. A delightful and fascinating book, in particular the twelfth chapter where fantasy and possiblility combine to provide a basis for thought and an urge toward doubt.

Index